KEEPERS
HOME & AWAY

ISBN 978-1-880977-51-4
Library of Congress Control Number: 2019954087

Distributed worldwide by Ingram Content Group
Available from independent booksellers and Amazon

Cover image photograph by Emily Zeller
Author photograph by Ed Kashi
Editing and cover concept by Pamela Hollie
Book design by Jerry Kelly

For my gangs — the Wiggin Street Coffee Corner, the Knox County Motorcross, the Kluge Hollie Garden Crew (founded by members of the Kenyon class of 1995) and the Radler Gang (Austria) — They All Have My Back!

402 Chase, Gambier, Ohio 43022

KEEPERS
HOME & AWAY

P.F. KLUGE

In a Word

If you're a writer, nothing is over until it's written down. Otherwise there's no encounter, no adventure, no love, no defeat or victory. Lost if not recorded. A writer's luggage comprises memories, which writing turns into keepers.

Personal Essays

The first section is personal. Almost, but not quite, private. "God, the Disc Jockey" is as close as I can come to religious belief. "Breakfast in Ohio" celebrates the best of what the countryside around my college offers. "The File Cabinet" and "My Private Germany" are about German-Americans residing in New Jersey — loyal Americans who never quite shed the link to the troubled nation, friends, relatives across the Atlantic, on the wrong side of history.

God, the Disc Jockey

Southwest Review, 2003

On a snowy morning, a few weeks before my sixty-first birthday, I walk across the campus of the college where I teach. The students aren't back from Christmas vacation and the place has an abandoned feeling, like a ghost ship, the Marie Celeste, sailing along without passengers or crew. I pass empty parking lots and sidewalks, empty bookshop and post office, everything empty as the branches of the trees, as the muddy fields of surrounding farms, vacancy and absence everywhere. And that is when I am ambushed, mugged, astonished by a song that comes to me from God knows where, out of the sky, out of the past, out of the ground beneath my feet or some fissure in the membrane that divides then and now. Even though there is no one around to hear me — perhaps because of that — I am humming, then I am singing "True Love Ways," a small gem of a song recorded by Buddy Holly shortly before his death in a plane crash more than forty years ago.

"True Love Ways" is a simple, slow lyric with none of Holly's trademarks, the rockabilly drive, the falsetto, the stuttering delivery. And it's by no means perfect; there is a dopey saxophone bridge that makes me wince. Still, "True Love Ways" is a quiet declaration of faith and love, faith in love, a last message from a musician who died young, a long time ago, who's been dead many years longer than he lived. The thought of him — the image of that doomed Texan with the heavy, horn-rimmed glasses — always moved me. Buddy Holly was over my shoulder when I wrote *Eddie and the Cruisers* twenty years ago; its themes were early magic and sudden loss. And now, on this wintry morning, he visits me again; not done with me yet.

"The day the music died," Don McLean called it: Holly, Ritchie Valens and The Big Bopper down in a cornfield outside of Clear Lake, Iowa, a snowy field, like the world I walk through now. Is that why the song found me? Or is it that I can see, from where I'm now standing, the place where I discovered that song? I came to Kenyon College in 1960, about two years after Buddy Holly died and, like ninety percent of Kenyon's all-male student body, pledged to join a fraternity. It lasted about a week, until I realized it wasn't for me. But on the night before I was gone, I sat downstairs in the fraternity lounge, a scuffed-up, ill-used place, pulling an all-nighter and I noticed a record player — that's what it was called — a turn-table and a speaker and just one record, which was "True Love Ways." What happened in the wee hours of that long-ago night was one of those times when you're so captured by a song that you play it over and over, not a couple of times, but a couple of dozen and with every playing you go deeper into it, it travels deeper into you. And so it happens, the song that finds a sixtyish writer in residence is the song that discovered a kid who was lonely in college, wondering about what he was doing there and whether he'd stay and who, a year later would apply for transfer to another, better-known school —Yale — and when the acceptance came, along with scholarship aid, decided after all to stay on the Ohio hilltop where he'd heard "True Love Ways."

I don't know why the song found me, back then, or why it returns on this particular morning, though I can speculate about how the weather, the landscape, the empty campus conduce to memory. But I'm sure of one thing: the song found me, I didn't find it. In a moment of random magic it came back to me, an oldie but goodie, a touch from the past. It's an odd linkage and it's happened before, not always and not often, but often enough.

People and places in my life are connected to — until just recently, I'd have said embedded with — songs that don't go away. Since many songs are love songs, it comes as no surprise that people I've loved, a little while or longer, have songs attached to them. A song by Bobby Vee, a minor singer, a Holly imitator —"Like a Rubber Ball, I Come Bouncing Back to You" — recalls a girl I dated, on and off, all through high school. Thomas Wayne's one hit wonder —"Tragedy" — brings back a pleasant twinge of pain. And something by a man named Gordon Keith called "I'll Try to Please You" summons up a woman, the woman, who broke my heart when I was in graduate school at the University of Chicago. I might be the only person who brought that record — three of them, in fact, three 45 r.p.m.'s. I was determined not to lose that song, even though I lost the woman. These days, I don't own a record player — a turntable, that is — but those records are in the house, packed away someplace and I would feel awful, it would be like a little bit of death, if they weren't around. And now, if you want to know which song is my wife's, I would say none. Or many. Elton John's haunting "Blue Eyes" might be it, enough though my wife's eyes are definitely brown. Songs connect us to our past and my wife is past and present. The perfect song is out there, I'm sure, I just haven't decided yet. The hits just keep on coming.

More than people, places come trailing songs — or are announced by them. It goes both ways, the song brings back the place or the place brings back a song. Consider a certain song — it still gets played a lot — that, whenever I hear it, carries me back to the south side of Chicago and the Regal Theater, where the opening act at a rhythm and blues road show was a group I'd never heard of, four gents in dark suits who looked like they had no business in front of a restless and noisy mid-afternoon crowd. Their jazzy version of "Teahouse In Old Chinatown" went nowhere fast and their next offering failed to impress. This wasn't a patient audience. But then — I still get goosebumps when I think about it — a surge of music came out of the Red Sanders Orchestra and it was joined by something else that I've heard a thousand times since — woo-woo-woo-woo-woo ooh ooh, roughly — and it was a miracle at 47th and South Park, the Regal Theater lifting off the ground, the guys in leather coats and stringy-brim hats, the women in the white uniforms of nurses, maids, waitresses, and me — all of us levitated by The Four Tops' "Baby, I Need Your Loving." When I hear that song, I'm back there and back there is now. Lives change, love drifts, addresses change, but the music hangs around and keeps you whole. There was a Quonset hut I stayed in from time to time on the Pacific island of Palau in the late sixties, Peace Corps days. A girl kept playing a Jimi Hendrix album so that his sinister "Hey Joe," surrounds me with greenhouse tropic smells, hot heavy air, night rolling in, rain drumming on the roof, just as "Come On Baby, Light My Fire" — Jose Feliciano's slow version, not Jim Morrison's — returns me to the island of Saipan, sweating out a hangover morning in a rotting wooden shack, conspiring to borrow someone's car — Kennedy's children, my Peace Corps generation, were supposed to stay on foot — so I could close a few bars after dark. And have I mentioned that on those rare occasions I hear Pete Wingfield's sneaky, dirty-minded "Eighteen, With A Bullet" I'm back on Saipan because that's what Casey Kasem was playing on Armed Forces radio when my wife and I parked under a row of soft-needled pines before swimming among rusted breakwaters and sunken barges left over from World War II at a place called Charlie Dock? Or how I as out west, jogging on a side road off Topanga Canyon Boulevard and there were some carpenters — young guys, sun-tanned California pagans — hammering a deck onto a house and all singing along with the radio, which was playing The Skyliners' magnificent "This I Swear." Do you think that just happened by accident? One more, please. I used to drink at a long-since closed bar/brothel called The Spider's Web on Del Pilar Street in Manila. When the theme from Flashdance, Irene Cara's "What A Feeling" or Paul Young's "Every Time You Go Away" came out of the jukebox, the hostesses up and down the bar would pick up the chorus and it was sing-along-time in the red light district, because whatever happened, they still believed the lyrics of the popular songs. And so do I. Still.

The list goes on. Life adds to it, even as the songs themselves enrich life. What's important is that the songs come to me, as they wish. I don't arise, intending to remember a song. I can't plan what I'll recall. I'm at the mercy of something I don't understand, just a receiver. And though it's tempting to say I'm a sensitive and willing receiver, I have no way of knowing what transmissions other people are getting. I'm like a jukebox with a lot of buttons waiting to be pushed, but it's anybody's guess how the buttons on my jukebox compare with anybody elses'. My father had a button or two. Walter Kluge was a (mostly) cheerful agnostic who was nonetheless moved to tears by arias in Italian operas, especially La Boheme, which I cannot listen to — thanks to my old man — without weeping some myself, tears running in the family. All through it. My mother Maria Ensslen Kluge wasn't much of a believer, though she would have liked to be. Yet I can't forget finding her in the kitchen nook, looking out at the garden, crying while the radio played Patti Page's treacly hit, "Throw Momma From the Train." You might think it's pathetic, probably bathetic, especially if you saw the dark-humored Danny DeVito film that took the song title literally, contemplating matricide. But terrible as it was, the song's lyrics pictured throwing a kiss to Momma from the train. That's what got my mother. When she heard that song, she was back in Stuttgart in 1923, on a train sliding out of the Hauptbahnhof. It was the first leg of a trip that would bring her to Ellis Island. Left behind on the platform was the mother she would never see again. So maybe everyone is reached this way once in a while. Some people have small jukeboxes, like the ones you see in diners, that you can never turn up as loud as you'd like — and other people have those mighty glowing Wurlitzers you find in roadhouses and old taverns with dozens of tunes, some from last week, others from decades ago, the titles written in hand, the ink long faded, but it's somebody's favorite song that you'd better not mess with.

Who's pushing the buttons? That's the question. Who's transmitting? Are these music-encoded memories, these memory-bearing songs mere random hits, like transient snatches of communication we keep hoping for from outer space? Or — I put the question carefully — is there something out there? And in us? Does God come into it in some way? And, if so, could the god I picture be something like the disc jockeys of my youth who were god-like figures in their own way, unseen movers, disembodied voices, heavenly voices transmitting across time and distance to a ready and faithful listener?

Martin Block was the first, out of New York City — I was in New Jersey, twenty miles west of the Holland Tunnel — and what he played was pure 1950s, pre-rock-and-roll. The only song I remember was the show's theme: "It's the make-believe ballroom time, the hour of sweet romance." The real music was in his voice, suave, confident, "continental." I kept wondering what Martin Block looked like, if the rest of him matched his voice. When I saw him — it must have been an early TV appearance — I learned the answer was no: he was a natty man with a thin mustache that was out of style even then. Martin Block looked like a haberdasher — equally out of style — and just as certain film stars couldn't transit from silent films to talkies, Martin Block was a voice that couldn't be satisfactorily incarnated. It was good that gods and DJs work out of sight, I thought.

Wolfman Jack was something else again. Holed up in a mega radio station across the border from Del Rio, Texas, the Wolfman mixed gravelly black evangelizing, plugs for live chickens and for Jesus pictures that glowed in the dark, with songs by early rhythm and blues groups, the Coasters, the Olympics, all those bird groups: Ravens, Penguins, Meadlowlarks, Orioles. "Get naked children," he preached. "When you're naked, you're closer to the lord." By the time I met him, he'd already been canonized by an appearance in *American Graffiti,* and his career had gotten... well, complicated. I was subpoenaed after an interview I did with him; there was some kind of dispute between him and his manager which I was supposed to be able to clarify. The Wolfman was a hustler, an Italian American guess, who confessed to being born in New Jersey, pimping in Baton Rouge, Louisiana, dodging bullets in Mexico before winding up — and down — in Los Angeles. He was an imperfect man to say the least and that as such he could have meant so much to so many kids suggests there was a whiff of divinity in his carny act.

But the greatest disc jockey of all was someone I never saw, he was only a voice in the air on a Jewish-owned black-staffed radio station. WVON — "Voice of the Negro" — that kept me company on the loneliest Saturday nights I ever had during my first months of graduate school at the University of Chicago in 1967. His name was Herbert Rogers Kent, Herb "the Cool Gent" Kent, and he was with me when I sat in my room at the International House, not knowing anyone, not sure where go, waiting for a new chapter to begin. The Cool Gent saved me. He was a dazzling monologist something like Jean Shepherd, but Shepherd was a writer. Kent was a talker, his beautiful words were here and gone as the wind that blew down the Midway, the steam that came up from manhole covers, that fluttered and floated and vanished. For the Cool Gent, I have only memories to count on. The Cool Gent wrapped his riffs in songs — Chicago soul, rhythm and blues, doo-wop, Curtis Mayfield and the Impressions, Jerry Butler, the Five Stair Steps, Billy Stewart, Walter Jackson and some very local groups like Baby Huey and the Babysitters. Every song trailed memories, generated stories, tone poems about high school dances, old flames, lost friends, "some fine hammer from DuSable High School." The Cool Gent was a poet, his very voice changed the way you looked at the unprepossessing, winter-sooty world around you, bare trees and frozen lawns, back alleys and fire escapes, the wind —"the hawk" — whipping around every corner; all of this the Cool Gent transformed into a land of magic, memory, and sexy possibility. That was what he did. Of all the disc jockeys, he was the poet and the poet, Philip Sidney contended, was prophet, priest, and king.

What comes next is hardest and anyone who thinks I make too much of these songs, these evanescent melodies, anyone who suspects I have stared too long in my life's rear-view mirror and that, bottom line, I am — as we say in New Jersey — carrying six pounds of shit in a five pound bag — had better stop here. For my largest conjecture is about to come. And I put it, with no disrespect, and with no intention to blaspheme, in the form of a question: if it's possible to attribute god-like qualities to disc jockeys, might it be possible, even desirable, to picture god as something of a disc jockey as well?

We live, as is well known, in an imperfect world. Carry on as I do about music and memories, and yet, if we add them all up, these K-Mart epiphanies, they are far outweighed by the patches of silence and static in our life. In a perfect world, an omnipotent god at the helm, our lives would be like movies, with a continuous sound track. The music would have us covered, Super Dolby, wall to wall, a note for every step, a note for every breath we take. The theme from *Rocky* would trail me when I slipped into my sweat pants and stocking cap and went running. And Tex Ritter's version of "Do Not Forsake Me, Oh My Darling," the theme from *High Noon,* would escort me into faculty meetings. The Ronettes' "When I Saw You" would be in the air, along with the whiff of a hot meal, when I welcomed my wife at the end of a long day. But life's not that way; mostly, we get noise. Now I'm aware that God gets credit for those long un-magical passages when he withdraws. They tell me this is unsupervised recreation, free-will time, when we establish God's godliness and our humanity by screwing up. Clever stuff. And if the idea of a passive-aggressive deity hanging at the edge of a playground listening for the first four-letter word appeals to you, feel free. But before you go, consider God, the disc jockey, operating from a mighty transmitter across many time zones and borders — we're talking way out there at the mercy of bad weather, mutinous equipment, sunspots — and, as a rule, better received at night. Picture God at some heavenly console, sending music out to all of us, but the playlist is finite and the audience is infinite, God's time is forever and our time is short. Is it any wonder that we only hear from God now and then? That what we get is occasional music on no fixed schedule, now tantalizing, then mocking, and sometimes so right-on it can break your heart. And granted, it lacks the constancy of opera, it lacks the careful patterning of classical music, adagios and allegros duly placed and please, no applause between movements, it lacks the fidelity of Hollywood soundtracks, John Williams or Jerry Goldsmith following you around like a dog on a leash. God, the disc jockey, is only sometimes on the air. That is why we have to keep listening. That is why, when I take long car trips, I avoid the cassette and CD players my friends carry along, for this preempts what should be left to a higher power. It presumes too much. I take my chances on the radio, on whatever's out there, suffer through farm prices and talk shows, keep myself available for a song that might be headed my way. I can't make it happen, but I can be ready if it does. If it doesn't, I'll understand. God, the disc jockey, contends with advertisements, news, public service spots. It is not, we need to be reminded, all about us. Not that we ever learn. Consider the requests that arrive from God, the DJ's listening audience. This isn't about Donna from West

Orange dedicating Whitney Houston's "I Will Always Love You" to Josh in Tenafly, no way. This isn't about first love, old love, breaking up and making up. These requests to God are urgent, concerning tumors and wars, famine and plague, children dying, every play-this-for-me a prayer, a matter of life and death. It's not an easy job and it doesn't surprise me if God the DJ has some yeah, well, whatever days. If God can't knock off early some days, who can? For some time, I've suspected that, like his — or her — earthly agents, God the DJ doesn't personally respond to every incoming prayer, i.e. please play "Wild Thing" for all the guys down at Jiffy Lube. My hunch is that if God the DJ feels like playing "Wild Thing," or better yet, "I Believe in Miracles, Where You From, You Sexy Thing?" that's what gets played. An underling finds someone who requested that song. How, really, could it be otherwise?

All of this may seem wishful. People more strenuously concerned with their spiritual lives may find what I've said less rigorous than they like. I don't disagree. What I offer in God the DJ is less a profession of faith than an expression of hope. So call me wishful. In the end I may be disappointed but my life is richer for having hoped. Those moments of contact with the DJ upstairs are as close to heaven as I've come. Whether there is such a place and whether I get to it is another, less interesting, subject; the journey, not the destination, was always the point. So the moment may or may not come, on the other side, when the music grows louder, clearer, finer as I get closer and what I hear is Buddy Holly's "Not Fade Away" and the Rolling Stones' "Time Is On My Side" and Ben E. King's "Stand By Me"— sung slowly, please — and for my wife — Jerry Butler's "For Your Precious Love." This is what I hoped it was all coming to — to God, the disc jockey — and if it doesn't work out, it was what I loved in the world I left behind, taverns with great jukeboxes and good friends.

Breakfast in Ohio

Antioch Review, Spring 2004

If I were never to see Ohio again, the house I live in, my garden, the small college where I teach, it's these mornings I would miss the most: these Saturdays and Sundays when my wife and I roll out of bed before eight, climb into my truck, and head out into the country for breakfast.

I can defend where I live — Gambier, Ohio, a small college town, an hour north of Columbus — in all sorts of ways: for its closeness to some things, its remoteness from others, as well as for some intrinsic virtues like the play of seasons over the Kenyon College campus, the river of life that flows through a place that is half Grovers Corners, half Mount Olympus. I can defend the place, all right. But not the food. "I've consulted the records closely," I tell Kenyon's incoming freshmen every August. "And the records are clear. No one has ever come to this part of Ohio because the food was good." That gets a laugh, but live here a while and it's not funny. If you go out to eat after dark in Ohio, if you're hoping for more than pizza or hamburger, you're risking heartbreak: brown meat, underdone potatoes, boiled-to-death vegetables. Coffee is a weak and see-through off-brown fluid, and as for pie, as in the stale slogan, "leave room for pie," it only rarely and only in season begins to atone for the waste of money and calories that precedes it.

Ethnic restaurants — Italian and Chinese about cover it — provide little relief: canned tomato paste and sticky-sweet hot and sour sauces, laced with pineapple chunks. You can only wonder whether these people are adulterating and diluting their food because they think that this is what customers want in the Buckeye State, and whether all the while they sit laughing in the kitchen, inhaling savory, pungently spiced meals they prepare for themselves. Or have they been so long in the diaspora that they've forgotten what things are supposed to taste like? Is this the meaning of the melting pot? Forgetting how to cook? It's hard to know. The problem, bottom line, is that though some people believe that, when you eat out, you order dishes that require ingredients, equipment, styles, and skill Mom's kitchen lacks, in Ohio they order — and get — more of the stuff they don't feel like cooking at home. Leave room for pie.

Then there's breakfast in Ohio, which I love. It's the only meal that comes naturally, the only dining occasion that doesn't seem forced and artificial. The drive to breakfast is crucial, the half hour that takes us out into what is still farm country, fields of corn and soybean, sheep and cattle, meadows and pastures topped by wooded hillsides. The streams around here are called "runs" and, like the roads, have local names that show up in graveyards, in election campaigns, and on the maintenance, security, and secretarial rosters at Kenyon College. As we drive to breakfast in Ohio, I'm reminded of long-ago car trips with my parents, who left home early and always waited, until the wait was almost unbearable, another ten minutes, another ten miles, until we stopped for breakfast and ordered what my father called "the works," orange juice and all. Then as now, breakfast was a reward and, as I think of my parents now, backing out of the driveway, gravel crunching under our tires, riding on a surge of joy, it was a communion.

There's a place in Bladensburg, a dozen miles south of campus, that serves something called "the ultimate omelet," which my wife and I split. It takes a while to arrive; that's because of the potatoes. We insist on well-done potatoes rather than the half-cooked, room-temperature product most places serve: poor pre-shredded stuff that looks as if it were extruded from a pipeline. The waitress warns the kitchen to fire things up as soon as we walk in, but there's still a wait. We don't mind. We study the street outside — State Route 62 — and the houses across the street, some peeling clapboard, others sided with vinyl and, vinyl aside, there's nothing in front of us on those crowded, sociable porches, these lawns patrolled by dogs and toys, that couldn't belong to the America of the Eisenhower years. Or even earlier: the ghosts of Sherwood Anderson's Winesburg, Ohio, hover here. What became of the smartest student who ever graduated from a local school, the most beautiful or handsome kid, the legendary delinquent? Did they leave and were they better off for leaving? Or stay? Is homesickness a disease people catch anymore, or has it died out in America, like mumps?

Fifteen miles east of Kenyon, just outside the Knox County line, there's Newcastle, which anyone would have to say has seen better days. Abandoned homes— tear-downs — line the main street, along with places that used to be gas stations, stores. Only two commercial establishments survive. One is a strip joint called The Foxhole, which advertises "Toppless" Dancing. The other is a breakfast place once known as The Derrick Inn, in the days they drilled oil around here. Later it was Monty and Gayle's, now it's Peggy Sue's, which we like most in autumn when hunters in camouflage crowd the place and sometimes you can see a wild turkey in the back of a pickup truck. But Bladensburg and Newcastle, good as they can be, are changes of pace. Our main retreat is north.

The Whiffletree Restaurant in Butler is farthest from campus, but the drive there — half an hour or so — is pure Ohio, the good, the bad, the ugly. It's a pleasure to escape from Mount Vernon, where the downtown of brick streets, town square, century-old buildings has been drained by a highway murderer's row of discount stores and fast-food franchises. Within a few miles we're in the country, thank God, among hobby farms, horse farms, Amish farms, falling-down farms, and there are a few places along the road that are so fine, we slow down to a crawl, and if anyone's behind us, pull to the side and let them pass, so that on Proper Road we can check on one place that uses a fiberglass boat as a planter and another that has an artful roadside garden. On North Liberty Road, just past Shady Lane, the road lifts a little and you're all of a sudden in big-sky country, a vista of farms and fields that rolls on for miles. And, on the same road, there's a secret place where a brook winds through a grove of trees, cattle pasturing on the banks, every bit of it out of an illustration in a children's book. This is when we feel lucky to live in Ohio and those mornings drives are patrols, really, making sure our luck hasn't changed. But, halfway to breakfast there's a place we hate — "time to close your eyes," I say to my wife. "I'll tell you when to open." It's not that closing your eyes does any good; we both know what's going on, here and there and everywhere. First, it's a row of signs along the road, evenly spaced the way Burma Shave advertisements used to be, Lot One, Lot Two, Lot Twelve, Lots A through J, another farmer selling off his frontage. Then it's gravel driveways cut into the fields. Next — and this can happen in the time it takes me to grade and return a pile of student papers — the homes appear, manufactured homes, assembled on site, trailers without wheels basically, though there are plenty of wheels parked outside, two to four per cubicle, new, used, and dead. When we see those acreage for sale signs — an outfit called "Country Time" is a prime vendor — it's as if we've gotten bad news from a doctor about someone we love. Still, the worst hasn't happened, not yet, and when my wife opens her eyes it's farms and fields again and then we're slowing down as we come into Butler, "The Core of Johnny Appleseed Country."

At the Whiffletree Restaurant, some mornings are better than others. We count the pickup trucks outside, the more the better, and if cars compete with trucks we know we've come too late. A second count follows as soon as we're seated, and I have to say that my wife counts along with me and for the same reason. We count the number of men in the room and then the number of women, which on some days takes no time at all; there are eighteen, twenty, two dozen men enjoying breakfast or lingering over coffee. No women. A dozen regulars sit around a long table that fills, partially empties, shifts and refills, like the cups of coffee the waitress keeps pouring. Now Lisa, the regular waitress, approaches us. As usual we're sitting as close as possible to the regulars. Lisa is patient and long-suffering. I'm always asking for what isn't there; that is my nature. So I inquire about eggs benedict, scrapple, grilled trout, creamed spinach, and creamed chipped beef and then, as usual, choose between French toast with sausage and/or bacon or corned beef hash with a poached egg on top and oh, yeah — I can see Lisa brace — a side order of potatoes. And now our litany: "Eye contact, please,"

I say. Sometimes she looks up from her order pad, sometimes not. "Those potatoes?" I ask. "They need to be well done: Crisp. Brown. Charred —"

"Incinerated, incarcerated," she responds.

Now that potatoes — the Waterloo of American short order restaurants — are under control, I turn back to that table of regulars, effortlessly, freely enjoying each other's company. I know their faces pretty well by now, but not their names. There's a small, dapper man who fusses with his hair; a lumbering, soft-spoken guy who brings his granddaughter to breakfast sometimes; and a chunky man who ordinarily wears overalls and flannels until the weekend rolls around in early autumn, when he shows up in the black shorts and black and white striped shirt of a football official. They're familiar figures by now; I'm used to seeing them and they're used to me. When we enter, I get a glance, maybe a nod. Which is nothing compared to what they get from me, the way I listen — eavesdrop, catching snatches of sport talk, stock talk — it could be stock as in stock market or stock as in livestock — hunting talk, fences, trucks, weather. And, because they're all middle-aged or more, there's talk of someone going in or coming out of the hospital down in Columbus, someone cut open or sewn up. I attend to the ebb and flow of conversation, a jocular argument, a challenge, a relapse into private chats, then a return to something loud and playful that dominates the whole table.

Where are their wives? Were these guys chased out of their homes or did they flee? Did they jump or were they pushed? Another question: What would it take for me to join them, to find a place at the regulars' table? Like a kid eyeing a girl at a party, I plan my line. "Say, can anybody help me, I need some cowshit for my garden." Or maybe: "I was wondering where I could find a free-range chicken." What if, like them, I managed to run from, or be run off by, my wife one morning? Or, just once, and only in the interests of science, I left her sitting out in the truck awhile? I walk in, genuflect at the John Wayne painting, nod at Dave and Debbie, the owners, greet them by name even, pass on the incarcerated, incinerated routine with Lisa, decide this is the day for biscuits and gravy, and then: "I'll just sit with these guys, if it's okay —"

There's no way it'll ever be okay. I can't picture it and, if I can't picture something happening, something that involves me, at least, then it can't happen. About a yard separates me from the regulars' table, just enough room for a waitress to pass, but it might as well be the English Channel. I'm a regular guy, I tell myself; I follow sports, I crack jokes, I listen to oldies but goodies, I'm from New Jersey, and when it comes in handy I tell people I'm working class, at least my father — a machinist — worked in a factory, whatever he might think of the college professing I get paid for now. Still, there's no way I'm getting to that table and now, in mid-morning, when the table thins out and the number of women showing up for breakfast increases, I realize that even if just one coffee drinker were left behind, even if the whole table were empty, I could not find my place there.

At the end of breakfast in Ohio, as we wait for someone to come to take our money, I wander into a gift shop that's in an alcove behind the cash register, looking for Dale Earnhardt, the tragically killed race-car driver. Ohio, you see, is a womb of yard ornaments — "yardos" for short. There are five-foot cutout figures of pipe-smoking men leaning against trees, painted wooden women in polka-dot bloomers bending over to pull weeds. There are white-painted truck tires, half-buried metal bedframes, transplanted toilets, all used as planters. Most of all, there are fifty-pound, cast-concrete geese that locals dress up for Christmas, Halloween, the Fourth of July, for summer heat and winter frosts, fair weather and foul, the wardrobe always changing. And here is a clothing store for geese, with dresses, bonnets, pinafores, tunics, many of them with pleats, lace, frills, ornately detailed, clothing to fit all sizes from oven-stuffer adults to tender goslings. And there's one item I've had my eye on for years, and though I haven't got the heart to buy it, I have to make sure that no one else has claimed it, a simple black-white-red tunic with letters spelling out EARNHARDT across the back. A yardo-goose in front of a professor's house: another thing I can't picture.

Our drive home is meandering, thoughtful. Our college town can wait while we test new roads, fill the back of our truck with flats of plants, with apples and cider, wreaths and honey we find along the way. That long table bothers me, all the way home. It's not just that I can't join that table at the Whiffletree. What bothers me more is that in the place I am going to, which I call home, it is equally impossible to picture such a table.

As we head home from breakfast in Ohio, driving from College Hill to Pealer Mill, through Jelloway and tiny Amity, that table which I cannot join in Butler and cannot fill in Gambier grows more important. I muse on the place of the table in history, literature, film, beginning with the first table — the last supper, that is — final meeting of God and man, a gathering of loyalists, all but one, and martyrs to be. There are movie tables that angry, divided juries sit around for hours, sweating out guilt and innocence, or tables where generals sit, Dr. Strangelove in his underground war room, and then the tables of a hundred Hollywood dinner parties where — you can count on it — something will be spilled, the beans or the wine. I think of long tables in prisons where riots erupt, in college dining halls, where food is wasted, played with, and complained about. Now I realize what those men at the Whiffletree Restaurant have is one of the rarest things in the world, and one of the nicest: a cheerful table of people regularly enjoying each others' company. What do those guys have — or lack — that enables them to meet this way? And what do we college people have — or lack — that keeps us from doing the same thing? We're nice people, aren't we, and we live in a nice place. People envy our rustic surroundings, our park-like hilltop campus, our paths and benches. You can see it in their eyes when they drop off their kids at the start of school. Our life is good: here is where you can contemplate the big questions. But my big question — that empty table — remains.

A small residential college is a sociable place, granted. That is how we think of ourselves: human-scale, personal touch, justice tempered by mercy. That is what we are and what we sell. See your professor in class, of course, and during office hours, if you wish. That's just the start. See your professor on the sidewalk of our block-long village, at the bookstore, the bank, the post office, at athletic events, on the running trail. The contact — the contract — we offer is unlimited. And a lot of contact occurs, it's true. I enjoy having students on my property, picking tomatoes, pitching horseshoes. I like having students on my porch, watching evening roll in, or in my house, splitting a pizza, attending Friday night boxing matches. I like having students in my life, current students or, better yet, graduates who turn every reunion weekend into a marathon walk down memory lane. Students are there for me. The problem of the table, as I come to think of it, arises in regard to adults, college faculty and administrators.

A small residential college is a company town — that's the first answer that occurs to me. People who work for the college live up and down my street. The college is the only game in town and spousal (or partner) hiring is a drama as endless, and repetitive, as a daytime soap opera. A majority of the faculty not only work at close quarters, we live in them as well. The sort of rampaging assaults you saw in *Who's Afraid of Virginia Woolf,* the over-the-top vendettas on display in *Straight Man* or *Lucky Jim,* cannot be accommodated in Gambier, Ohio. Do or say something unforgivable and you' re bound to encounter your target at the post office, in line at the movies, raking leaves. Face it: crime rates go down when victim and perpetrator are obliged to remain at the scene of the crime, forever. Extreme states — love and outright hate — are risky here and the result is a paradox. Proximity can lead to familiarity, but in faculty it generates a contrary movement, self-protective and desperate, toward distance. As long as you're on campus, you're on stage, you're performing in front of an audience. You not only fill a role, you incarnate an approach to life, and the room left for private endeavor can shrink to almost nothing. Before long, a university-trained scholar with a fresh Ph.D. begins to feel he or she has returned, not to college but to a prep school, right out of *Goodbye Mr. Chips* or *Dead Poets Society,* which isn't what they'd planned. Some smart and worthy people adapt to, even welcome, college life; in others ambition dies hard, that old all-out dream of publication, performance, recognition in the world outside. The tension between what we are and what we meant to become, where we are and where we meant to go, is inevitable. The promises we make to ourselves are the hardest to keep, or break. They're what haunt us.

There's more. Though they're accustomed to holding forth in front of students, many professors are reticent, even awkward on the even playing field of the Sunday breakfast table. You can't picture them there any more than you can picture them at a tavern or a wrestling match. Students confirm this. When they spot us at an airport or in a distant city, they're shocked: "Holy shit, I didn't know he left campus." We're figures in a landscape, insects in their memory's amber, stationary and discrete. What this all comes to is, I can't imagine my colleagues spending weekend mornings at breakfast together. If asked, they'd demur. If required, they'd howl.

It's a non-starter, my idea of a long table in a college town. Its death, by now, is over-determined. It has to do with academics, not with the absence of friends but of a certain style of friendship. We don't mix the way other people do, we don't go back as far or stay as close. My wife and I could make a list of names, terrific people, enough to fill a table. And we could spend hours deciding who should sit where. We'd have a dozen people in a dozen chairs all right, a fine evening. But it wouldn't happen again, not soon, and it wouldn't happen on its own, without our asking. So, I will continue to head out into the country on Saturday and Sunday mornings, heading to Bladensburg, Newcastle, or Butler, celebrating the life I have and the life I missed, just down the road.

The File Cabinet

New England Review, Fall 2002

The wooden cabinet is rickety and ancient and at night, when I watch television, it makes creaking sounds, expanding and contracting with the weather, warning that if we ever move to another house, it will stay behind. It was old when we found it, in a Los Angeles antique shop. The cabinet was English, the dealer told us, used for the storage of World War One medical records. As veterans died, the drawers were emptied. For the past quarter century — and until someone I don't know empties the drawers out again — the file cabinet has contained records of the more recently dead: my family. My mother died in 1969 — my years without her far out-number those we shared. My father followed in 1975, my Uncle Fritz in 1987. Like so many stones dropped into a deep pond, they fall further away each day. Yet the ripples of their lives reach out to me: That is what the filing cabinet holds.

Summer comes to the campus I call home, an empty student-free campus, succulent and sullen, and this is when I keep my appointment with the past. I open the drawer on the bottom right. Some of what I find inside is mine, an eighth grade autograph book, a boxing program from the Olympic Auditorium in Los Angeles. These things of mine are aging along with the papers I'm looking for. The same stream of time that carried my elders off is moving me along as well. Soon I find what I'm looking for and take it to my office, where family photographs are on the wall, photos I've been looking at for so long that when I think of my parents, my uncle, all the rest of my relatives — "the whole kit and caboodle" — it is these photographs that come to me, black and white stills. I have photos of Christmas celebrations, summer beer parties, trips to Jones Beach or Florida or Germany, where they were born and kept returning, one more trip, always one last trip. One last trip is what I'm taking when I reach across the desk, see familiar handwriting, vivid as a voice and memorable as the smell of my own sweat.

I. Pop's Book

A retired machinist, living twenty-miles west of the Holland Tunnel, my father wrote his life story in the mid-1960's. Fifty-seven pages long, typed out by a next door neighbor. *This Is My Life* is the longest and most ambitious of the family papers I have. Also, the most public. My father had a sense of audience, the family that would survive him. And, I'm pretty sure, he had a sense of me. I was a puzzling kid in many ways, bored by garden work, useless when not dangerous around tools. But the old man watched me work on newspapers, go to college and major in English, whatever that meant, go on to graduate school and get to be called a doctor, not that you could bring me anything that hurt or bled. Well, I was smart, maybe. But he'd been smart longer. If I could write, so could he. If Freddy could do it, how hard could it possibly be? There was something else too. He believed that his life mattered. His disclaimer notwithstanding — "Why do I bother, after all I am not an important person." — he sensed a story that needed telling. "I was the first one to cross the ocean and start a new life over here," he writes. "Let me try to tell you all about it."

What follows is straightforward, choppy, lively, opinionated and digressive. In the early going it is interrupted by accounts of friends and relatives who pop up, take a bow and disappear. Later years are dominated by car trips, ocean cruises and trips back to Germany. Still. My old man has his moments. In and between the lines, the lifelong love of three places emerges. The first was Hamburg, where he was born in 1903. His father was a tinsmith, his mother kept a small grocery store. Early memories are vivid: Christmas, his first day at school, standing in food lines during World War I, scavenging the streets for manure for the family garden. There are delicate moments: he recalls the nightly promenade, up and down the street outside his window, of a man with a long stick, reaching up to pull a lever that ignited the gas lamps of Hamburg-Altona. In winter, he loved hopping from one chunk of ice to another along the Elbe. He boarded at an outlying farm while his father served the Kaiser in Alsace-Lorraine. "Pop never fired a shot or harmed anybody."

Hamburg was a port city and the birthplace of his constant restlessness. He was a German without "sitzfleisch": he couldn't stay still for long. "The Elbe was a short walk from my home," he remembers, "and summer or winter I was always ready to go there… you could sit and watch the traffic in the river. The Elbe had a strong tide and as I grew up I knew at what time the tide came in. With the tide came steamers, sailboats, fishing boats with their brown sails. I think right here I got the wanderlust. How I wished to be on a fishing boat and go out into the North Sea on one of the big new ocean liners going all over the world…"

When he was young he imagined being a seaman. When he was old he wondered if he shouldn't have been a landscape gardener. He was a machinist, old-world trained, and there was always a factory that wanted him, even during the Depression. But he begrudged them every minute, spat on the wheels of the car he drove to work building printing presses. At home, his workbench was a mess, tools thrown everywhere, left where they dropped. In gardens, he was a joyful man. To watch him plant a hemlock seedling was to see his tenderest caresses. He wasn't that familiar around people, not much of a hugger or kisser and when someone told a dirty joke, he faked a laugh, blushed and turned away. He was shy that way, around women. "Those I wanted did not go for me," he writes, "and many others I had no interest in, so in this respect I was a very lonely boy."

In Germany, he spent the last year of the war and the first years of peace in a factory. After a dispute with a foreman — "trouble at work," is all he says — he left for an open-pit coal mine in southeast Germany, near the Polish border. "Here I was, not even nineteen years old and all by myself and a little worried about what to do next. The little village was covered with brown dust everywhere — trees, houses and streets... the countryside was ruined, nothing but sand, hills and holes... It was a terrible place."

In a company town where "you had two strikes against you for not being Polish," the teenager from Hamburg worked and saved. He was always careful with money, even in later years, when he didn't need to be. From a barracks where he slept with the lights on because bed bugs got busier in the dark, he sent money home. Worthless money, it turned out: runaway Weimar inflation turned his savings into waste paper. Rescue came from a relative he'd never met. Uncle Bruno Otto had left for the U.S. at the turn of the century, worked in a Michelin tire factory in New Jersey, quit when the plant converted to war production against Germany. By the 1920's he worked as a superintendent of a series of Manhattan apartment buildings. Every year, he brought a greenhorn over from Germany, giving them a year as a janitor in his building before they moved out into America. In 1923 my father's turn came, his life's first voyage, Cuxhaven to New York, with a night in Ellis Island.

"Next morning I was called into the reception room," he writes. "My papers were in order. I was told that my uncle was here. 'Can you see him?' I had never seen him except maybe a picture once, I am not sure. So looking around I see a man smiling at me and somehow I know that was him. The ferry brought us to the Battery and at nine o'clock that morning I stepped onto U.S. soil for the first time."

The next years of his life — two dozen pages of his story — are much the best. There's an openness to experience, a love of story: sleeping next to the boiler in the cellar, sharing space with a colored elevator operator who taught him English. "I can still see Larry laughing, grinning from ear to ear and at time almost going into a fit." My old man couldn't resist rummaging through the discards that came down the dumbwaiter, "almost new clothing," shoes with lots of wear left in them. He got his first suit off the dumbwaiter and a dozen pairs of ladies shoes. "At least some of them would fit my sister."

What I like about these pages is not that they reunited me with my passed-away father but that they carry me back to a time I couldn't share, a stretch of years I've only heard about. My parents were both 39 when I was born. I missed a lot. There he is stepping out of a machine shop at the foot of 138th Street, his first pay envelope in his hands and a pushcart loaded with fruit just outside the factory doors. "I liked bananas very much… so I bought a dozen of them and on my way home I ate every one of them." There he is in Brooklyn, renting an apartment with five other greenhorns, accommodating stowaways and illegal who drifted through. "If one of us had a girlfriend and wished to be alone with her, all he had to do was pay the movie admission for the other five." There he is, dark black hair, prominent nose, barrel-chested and bowlegged, cruising Eastern Parkway on a new motorcycle, crashing into the fence of the Brooklyn Museum, bribing a cop who asks to see his license. "I liked my job. I liked everything. Each walk I took, being very careful to remember how many blocks I was away from home, I saw something new..." There he is, meeting a German nanny wheeling someone else's baby in Riverside Park: my mother.

My father was a hectic worker, an on-time traveler, an outgoing talker. He sped through life, as though rushing to get to the ending of a book, to discover the moral, the meaning. No place could hold him: he was always planning the next trip. In 1924, the trip was from New York City down to Florida. Of all the trips he took without me, this is the one I miss the most. By the time I was in the car, in the 1950's, it was interstates all the way and the New Jersey state sport was seeing how fast you could escape to Florida: rest stops were pit stops, it was all about filling gas tanks, emptying bladders, and racing south in fast cars on fast roads. Back then it was different: the old man was discovering America, potholes, ferries, breakdowns. When he and a companion got to Jacksonville, they contacted my Onkel Hans, a shipboard musician who arranged for accommodation, food and shower on ship. On the last day of 1925, he drove down a narrow brick road called the Dixie Highway to Miami and the subtropical Florida he would love for the rest of his life.

"The first day in Miami, I thought I was in Paradise," he remembers, "warm sunshine, orange trees, grapefruit, bananas and flowers everywhere." He awoke at a relative's house, smelling fried pork chops and potatoes. He wrote to my mother, Maria Ensslen, to come down and on May 29th, 1926, they were married in the Miami Courthouse. Almost immediately, the dream of Florida fell apart for him. The Sunshine State was going from boom to bust and the factory he worked, manufacturing automobile spark plugs, quickly failed. They lived in a place called Lemon City. "Things got worse from week to week. I don't think my Maria was very happy out there in the middle of nowhere. We started to make a small garden but the sand all around us was not good for anything." Then a hurricane struck, not a bad one, but enough to send them north. "About twelve miles north of Jacksonville, I hit a wagon loaded with pine trees and pushed my radiator in," Pop says. "Somehow my brakes did not hold or I was too fast." They slept in the car and lived on hot dogs, limping north, stopping at rivers, wells, farmhouses to get water for the leaking radiator.

Hamburg was behind him, so was Florida, but only to the extent that he ever left anything behind. In fact, he returned again and again to Germany and considered moving back there in his old age. He died in Florida: the last picture I have of him, he stands next to an orange tree, beaming with pride, as if he'd hit life's jackpot. This pattern of returns runs in the family, the farewell tour, the last look, a presentation of your older self the places you knew and, more important, that knew you when you were young. Why else do I read his journal now, except to hear his voice, even just to be able to refer to him in the present tense, as if his ashes hadn't been scattered at sea — off of Florida — more than twenty-five years ago?

With his return north, my father becomes more like the man I used to know. After a 1927 trip back to Germany, the Kluges settled in Philadelphia where they lived in a small bungalow — all their houses were small — and worked a series of machinist jobs. My brother Jim was born in 1929, followed by two full-term and stillborn infants. I came in 1942. By then they were living in New Jersey, twenty miles west of Manhattan, in a rolling, wooded area that went from sticks to suburbs while I grew up. "Looking back for a moment," my father says, "the next 26 years we lived here were the happiest in our life. Here for the first time we had a home of our own, a great big garden to work in and a beautiful spot on top of the Watchung Mountains."

The years were good, I'm sure, but something drains out of Pop's writing in what amounts to the middle of his life. Maybe it's my fault, because this is where I came in, this is the part of the movie I saw. The fifties: my father's father sleeping upstairs, the Brooklyn Dodgers breaking my heart, the constant gardening that was so joyous to him, so tedious to me, squatting at the edge of the lawn, hand-clipping the grass along the sidewalk that the mower missed. Edward R. Murrow and Uncle Milty and the Friday Night

Fights, summer beer parties, onkels and tantes from three states coming down our driveway, horseshoes and German songs and listening to the men begin to wonder if the labor unions hadn't gone too far. But little of this is in his pages and that's the problem. He is a success story, a self-made paradigm, a man of opinions about the New York Yankees, the Catholic church. From the *Daily News* he's graduated to *The New York Times* and he likes to test himself against others, a "friendly exchange of views," always quoting Voltaire on disagreeing with others but defending to the death their right to speak. That Voltaire quote kept turning up ahead of arguments; the old man used it the way people say grace before a meal.

Now the early sense of wonder is in the past, the discovery of new places, the first taste of tropical fruit. Visits are summarized, relatives come and go, current events are stipulated. And so much is missed. My mother and father were Germans living in America while relatives fought and died in Hitler's armies. Two of my uncles were lost, another had his health ruined, a fourth — an SS lieutenant — was held by the allies for two years. My father's mother died in an underground hospital in February, 1945. How did it feel, when newsreels reported the incineration of Hamburg? And the world cheered while his loved ones were lost? "Our loyalty was never questioned," he says. "Of course having families over there was a constant worry for us but no one, at least in our family here or our circle of friends, was hoping for a victorious Hitler." Fine. I'm not looking for divided loyalties. But are mixed emotions too much to expect, intimations of pain and loss?

After the war, his traveling began in earnest, out west, down south, back to Germany. Reading about my father's travels tires me out. I remember how it was whenever we took a trip. I'd be sitting in the car and after a while my father would join me and both of us would be itching to hit the road. And my mother would linger behind, back in the house, staying behind forever, unaccountable, the morning draining away while we sat waiting at the starting line, hungry for breakfast down the road, eggs, bacon, orange juice and what was she doing inside. What's the big hold up? She was checking the doors, the windows, rechecking the stove, watering the African violets, walking through the house one last time to see "alles in ordnung" and what was out-of-ordnung was the horn-blowing from the driveway, which was my doing, though the old man could have stopped me, and both of us would be giggling when she came out of the house, furious or pretending to be. And then we hit the road, the two of them in the front seat, me in the back leaning forward, more than ready to cast a tie-breaking vote on where to stop for breakfast. Then or later, but not much later, when the idea of death came to me… of their deaths, that is… I pictured them driving forward in the car, talking now and then, watching the countryside pass by, the way they did when we went to Pennsylvania only I would not be with them, they'd be driving on — and away — without me. Actually, the trips without me already had begun, when school or summer jobs prevented me from joining them. They were already headed down the road.

My father traveled like a driven man and what propelled him was the search for something else, something he'd discount as the years rolled by. He went faster all the time, barreling through the years, his pace accelerating even as his descriptive powers thinned. They were captions for a slide show now; the language went flat. "Beautiful days" on a voyage from New York to Rotterdam, a pass in the Tyrolean Alps that was "perhaps the most beautiful spot I've seen," and then an evening in Venice, listening to music in St. Mark's Plaza, that was "a wonderful experience," after that "little Lichtenstein... very quaint." In 1959, Mitchell South Dakota, the Badlands, the Black Hills, Yellowstone, the Grand Tetons, Banff, Crater Lake Yosemite, a beautiful spot here, a wonderful something there, a world famous, colorful etc. etc., it goes on and on, pronouncements and endorsements, another trip to Germany in 1963, out west again in 1965 and then, in 1966 off to Germany again. "Our last trip," he calls it and he was half right. "Maria was twice more in the hospital," he writes. "A low grade cough was the reason each time. Twice a bronchoscopy and biopsy revealed no serious sickness and our doctor saw no reason to cancel or postpone the trip."

I remember my mother's cough, small and stifled, a kind of pleural hiccup that embarrassed her and annoyed my old man. Why can't you stop that, he seemed to say, giving her the kind of glare you aim to someone talking in a movie theater. He was retired now, escaped from the hated factory and what happens? What does she do? She gets this little nothing cough that doesn't go away.

"Had I only known what was going to happen," he writes, "had I known how sick my Maria was, I certainly would never have made this trip." He sounds defensive, on the edge of an apology which he retracts. "On the other hand, people told me why not — she had one more beautiful trip in her life. The point can be argued back and forth and we will never have the answer."

Madeira, Tangiers, Majorca, Sardinia, Geona, Canna, Monte Carlo, Barcelona: there's my father pressing forward, my mother trying to keep up and not ruin his dream. When he remembers her efforts his voice sounds strained and formal, the language of a deposition. "I do believe," he insists, "that Maria, up to this point, had enjoyed our trip but there was no change with her little cough. Her appetite and outward appearance was good, but long walks were out and the often windy weather with some dusty streets had to be avoided." Geneva, Roma, Florence, Venice and Germany at last, a spa town in the Black Forest where my mother's brother ran a bed and breakfast. "For our stay in Lenzkirch I had a lot of hope for Maria," Pop contends. "It was known for its healthy air, with pine forests all around us and, with a lot of resting in good air and sunshine, I thought she would surely be better soon." It was raining all the time, it seems, and Pop busied himself in his brother-in-law's garden, planting trees, while my mother stayed indoors. Their American doctor had suggested x-rays be taken in Germany. They went to Freiburg where one test led to another. "A week later Dr. Wohlfahrt told me, 'Mr. Kluge, your wife has cancer of the lung and has no more than a year to live.'"

"It will take time but you will get better," he tells my mother. They return early to the United States: bad weather is their excuse. Eight months after coming home, my mother is dead. Pop vows never to marry again, to have lost the fear of death, to take a renewed will to live on. And, on the last page of his life story, this bravado combines with an odd note of remorse. "Let me at this late date apologize to all of you I may have hurt in one way or another. Nobody is perfect, least of all me." I wonder who he has in mind. I can guess. He doesn't say and this is one of many places where I wish he had gone deeper. Sometimes, his journal brings out the professor in me. I could make a list of missed opportunities, evasions, avoidance. My mother is a shadowy figure, a mother, fellow-traveler, gardener, a good cook. What did he see, the first time he saw her. What... what on earth... did their courtship amount to? Did they fall in love? Every child has a hard time picturing parents as young lovers but my perplexity goes deeper. Does a concept of romantic love apply to them? Did they have it? Did they miss it? Does it matter? On love, on war, on death, my father is reticent. Too many large things escape him, and small ones too. His claustrophobia... which I share... blinding panic in confined places: he always wanted a seat on the aisle. His constant movement, movement as proof of life, working, walking, running; well into middle age he challenged me to foot races, sprints I never won. What about his moments of relaxation: how in winter we put chaise lounges on a concrete apron in front of the garage, where we lay down under blankets, tanning ourselves in what Pop called his "Florida room." And, on Sunday afternoons, full of roast pork (rind on, please), spinach and spätzle, he and I would lie down on the living room floor, on the carpet, napping with our rumps against the radiator. What about his odd love of opera, especially *La Boheme,* which I can't listen to without thinking of him. What about that time I came home from college with a beard. He glared, stormed, putted, offered me money to shave it off, ten or fifteen bucks. Hair as a cash crop. I refused. I tried to reason. I cited Christ, I cited Marx, all in vain. He couldn't be reasoned with. Till the morning when my mother's surprised shout interrupted my sleep. "Oh, Pop," she exclaimed. I jumped out of bed, rushed downstairs... was it a heart attack? —

and when I peeked into the kitchen nook, there was my father, holding his hands over his eyes, not wanting me to see him crying. The beard went that day. Being right wasn't everything.

All this is missing. Still, the manuscript doesn't fail, at least it doesn't fail me. Or him. Remember me, he pleads and I remember. I resisted looking at photographs while reading what he wrote. The whole point was to get past the photos, if that could be. But now I turn to four pieces of cardboard at the front of his journal, pictures of his parents' grave, his boyhood homes, the Elbe River, the school he went to and a nondescript cobble-stoned plaza. His handwritten caption breaks my heart: "In this little park, I played a lot." I remember the touch of his. A factory injury resulted in a raised, stiff tendon that kept a finger in a permanent crooked position that I ran my hand over when I was little. I feel it now. I remember his reading, mostly historical novels, *The Cruel Sea* and *Captain Blood* and the Horatio Hornblower series over and over again. I remember his coming home from a Jewish delicatessen in Plainfield with a pile of herring he'd cut and curl, shape into roll-mops he kept in a brine-filled clay pot that was in a cool cellar closet along with apples and onions. I remember how he organized our Boy Scout paper drives, nothing like it before or after, squads of kids moving from house to house, going into basements, tying up stacks of newspapers and magazines, carrying the bundles out to the curb for collection the next day. Fighting over nudist magazines. I remember my old man.

II. Mom's Book

"As I start this new book I wonder how everything and everybody is when it is filled up." The date is January 1, 1963, the handwriting is my mother's and the journal is a pocket-sized volume with a red leatherette cover and a metal clasp, a Christmas gift "to Mom from Fred, with love." It's intended as a one year diary but my mother made it last for nearly five and she left room when she stopped. It's her last diary and seeing it recalls what a lot of the German old-timers said, when they made a post-retirement purchase, a lawn mower, a suit, a car: "This will last me out." Said with a self-satisfied smile. "This will last me out." As if what was on display showed their lifelong shrewdness, not their imminent mortality. "This will last me out," not "This will outlast me." Control of the endgame, their last wish.

This is not the kind of journal you see creative writing students carrying around, filled with rampaging solipsism that not even a mother could love. Nor is it my father's autobiographical look backward, garnished with opinion and conjecture. These are the notes of a housewife writing a line or two at the end of the day, it's hard to say why or for whom, but there she was each night, in bed, making an entry before turning to her apple, her square of chocolate and an article or two in the Reader's Digest. Notes on who came to visit, on shopping and gardening and mail, on trips they took, with marginal asides on the cost of things, gas and tolls. When my parents took me to Kenyon College for instance: "We had breakfast at Howard Johnson, fair; lunch again at H.J. fair. The countryside is very nice."

Her early journals, trip journals, document the life I remember. But this last red-leatherette volume is darker. Sure, some entries are like what I enjoy remembering. "Another perfect day. I cut the grass and worked outside all day pulling weeds." Or, in May 1965: "Thirty eight years with my Pop." But age and sickness and disappointment start showing up. Love, too. But love isn't everything. And I'm at the center of it, whiplashes from page to page, generating feelings I never knew, pride and disappointment. It was a no-win situation. Like most mothers, especially — I suspect — immigrant mothers, she wanted me close, she wanted me happy, she also wanted me to go out in the world, the unfamiliar world of college, university, journalism, publishing and make her proud and marry a nice girl along the way. As soon as I was gone, whether for a year of college or a Saturday night in New York City, especially in notorious Greenwich (pronounced Green-witch) Village, her pain began. "A lonely day without my kid." "I miss Fred so much." "Took Fred to the airport; feel very lonely and blue." "Ho ist unser Junge?" She had my father at home, my brother and his wife a mile away. That only made things worse. Mom's expectations for letters and phone calls was endless, not just for communications but for intimacy, sharing, confiding. Consider a week in January, 1965. I am at the University of Chicago, cobbling together a Ph.D. thesis. I am worried about the draft and, though I have a generous fellowship, I'm not so sure about graduate school. I seem to be too academic for journalism and too journalistic for academe; this is a problem, by the way, I'm still trying to solve. Another thing: no love affair. And I tell all this to my mother, in her dreams. 1/5/65: "Fred did not call. I don't know whether to worry or be mad. Will he ever change? It's cold out." 1/6/65: "Still no mail from Fred." 1/7/65:

"Could it be that my kid just doesn't care. God it hurts." 1/7/65: "Fred just called and I am so relieved. He seems happy and got straight A's. Mild tonight."

When I came home she rejoiced. 3/21/66: "It is so nice to have my boy home." 3/22/66: "I wish I could turn back the clock and have my kid home again." 8/25/66: "It's wonderful to have our Fred home." The good feelings didn't last. 6/6/63: "Our Fred is so maladjusted." 6/11/63: "Fred is lonely and irritable." 9/7/63: "I can't find a way to reach my boy." Did she expect me to try out my Ph.D. thesis on her, my musing about American expatriate writers, on the paradox that as they left home they distanced themselves from their best work? Did she expect me to discuss finding a girl, a good girl, a bad girl, any girl at all? She looked perplexed when she caught me listening to doo-wop. Was an explanation required? And, I admit, when I picked up a book while lying on our tiny back porch it was more than once to shield myself from her hurt and wondering eyes. In her journal, I am most on stage but my old man comes in for collateral damage too. Though he holds forth in his memoirs on the waste of World Wars I and II, when Vietnam revved up he shared none of my doubts. 1/8/66: "I am terrible upset. Fred gets no more deferment and Pop does not understand. I swear all he thinks of is himself." and now, the beard. Forty years after I found him sobbing and shaved my senior-year-of-college-just-won-a-Woodrow-Wilson-Fellowship beard, I get mom's account of things. 3/14/64: "Fred came home around 8 p.m. with a beard. Pop is upset. Our first robin." 3/15/64: "I am very upset, not over Fred, but Pop." 3/16/64: "A very nice day. Pop is more like himself." 3/17/64: "Average day. Pop is getting around but I can't help feeling he is narrow minded about Fred." 3/18/64: "Fred shaved, thank God."

In 1964, she stops worrying about me so much. A series of small, stubborn physical complaints disturb her. 10/16/64: "I'm tired. Will I make the year?" She has a job as a cashier at the local high school cafeteria; she stubbornly persisted as her pains compounded, her leg, her back, that pesky cough. My father was exasperated. She was reneging on their retirement plans, jeopardizing their golden years. 3/12/65: "I don't feel good and am blue. Pop is impatient and I am hurt." 2/25/66: "It snowed all day. I cough a lot and Pop is upset over it." 4/6/66: "I am back in the hospital and sick at heart over Pop; he just cannot accept it." 3/14/66: "Pop painted at Mrs. L. He is so mad because I cough. I am disgusted with him. After all, I can't help it."

I can picture my hyperactive father escorting a neighbor woman to the movies, inventing errands, walking with neighbors, losing himself in his own and other people's gardens while my mother stayed inside. No wonder that last trip to Europe occurred to them, a change of scene, sunshine, piney air, a death sentence my father didn't share. "If Pop is telling me the truth, I should be satisfied."

Her last New Year's Day is January 1, 1967. "Hede made a delicious sauerkraut dinner and brought it down." Impatient when not in denial, my father does chores while mom charts her decline. I am in Chicago; a bound copy of my Ph.D. thesis sits on a bed table beside her deathbed. Mom continues her journal. For what purpose? For what audience? 1/4/67: "a nasty, foggy day." 1/7/67: "now my left arm hurts." Her handwriting is going, not the shape of the letters but their size — they've shrunk — and her pressure on the pen is lighter, the words are indistinct. 1/16/67: "I don't feel good my bladder." 1/26/67: "again it's my leg."

2/7/67: "we awake to snow again." 2/9/67: "my bones ache." 2/10/67: "very quiet, my back is bad." 2/15/67: "not so cold." 2/16/67: "I hurt again." 2/23/67: "more snow about 4"." Now her writing is faint and tiny. I can hardly make it out. 3/2: "Opa took Kathy to see 'My Fair Lady.' He liked it." 3/3/67: "warmer today but very boring." 3/10/67: "Dad took Fritz and Hede for a ride. I loved it." That is her parting line. She stopped writing then and died a month later. In her diary there was room enough for another two or three years.

III. Pop's Journal

There was one word that terrified him, ever since he learned its meaning when he was little. That word was never. He talked to me about it. Never was his death sentence, mine, everybody's. It suggested the finality of death, the total loss of everything. What claustrophobia did to his body, the word never did to his mind and spirit. He writes about it in an otherwise bland addendum to his earlier manuscript. "I will give you but one word," he says. "'Never.' Think about it, its real meaning. We use it so lightly every day. Never to see your family again, our children and all we love so dearly, never, never. Just think about it once in a while."

Now as each year brought him closer to the edge of never, my old man sold the house he built, lived briefly with my brother and his family — a mistake — then headed south to the New Jersey pine barrens, to a retirement community where a dozen friends and neighbors had settled. It was mostly a German place: you could tell as soon as you drove in off the highway and saw ceramic elves peeking at you from carefully tended yards. Life might have wound down comfortably in the Lakehurst walking along the nearby beach, fussing with postage stamp gardens, checking out the early-bird specials at local restaurants, waiting for visits from children, scrutinizing each other's health, and will the last one left please turn out the lights. The old man wasn't ready for that. He married again and this time he married a female version of himself, replacing my mother's depths and silences with Else Kaiser's hearty, strenuous cheer. My father was a talker. She talked more.

Now it was his turn to keep a journal of the sort my mother kept, several years of life compressed onto a page the size of a postcard. Unlike my mother's slanted tracings, my father's handwriting is spiked and upright. The back of the page feels like Braille, he pressed hard. They have one thing in common, though: their preoccupation with weather, highs and lows, rainy days and dry. Why all this fuss, I wonder. Then I get it. Weather is what they lived, the flow of days and years, their daily adventure, the very embodiment of time. 1/1/73: "Hi 80, lo 60, none (no rain). Nice warm day, had lunch and dinner on patio." One day after another, gardening, shopping, trips to the beach. Then he invents a new measure. The old man was sensitive to northerners' conviction that, inviting as it might be in winter, Florida was un-shirted hell from April to September. So he assessed the quality of each day. A perfect day was "100%." One follows another, they go on for weeks. "100% day watering. Cut the front hedge. Went for a dip." "100% day clear, went to ocean in morning beautiful." In June of 1975, his streak is broken. "Hospital." On June 10, he returns home, rushes out to the yard. "Lots of work, cut both lawns, watering." One "clear warm day" trails another, as if Florida were endorsing his decision to move there, to this little subdivision in Melbourne. In September he flies to Germany, visiting relatives, gardening on their property, walking in the Black Forest, taking a train to Hamburg where he visits his parents' graves. The next day, almost as if he expected something to go wrong, he writes: "Had a lot of pain. Time to go home. Feels like rheumatic but not sure." On September 30 he was back in Florida, on October 2. "Hospital again, what is it?" On October 4 he's upbeat. "Eats and nurses fine, all very friendly." October 5: "Can't pin it down." October 6: "I must be healthy all my organs work but still pain." On October 7, pop gets some good news. "It looks like arthritis." They send him home and he plunges into work, writing letters, transplanting crotons but the pains continue, over and now comes the saddest part because there's all that good weather out there, and it's like a party he can't join. October 13: "100% day I am sick." October 14: "100% day, had a bad day and night, such pains. October 17: "100% day the weather I mean but what a night." He goes to a chiropractor, an acupuncturist. October 26: "100% weather what a shame to stay home." He's going to a doctor every day now. It isn't his style, this discourse with doctors. The old man always avoided doctors. They cost and arm and a leg and for what? Mother Nature was the best doctor of all. One of us could come home with a half-severed arm, we used to joke, and the old man would say "It's okay, the body heals itself." He believed that illness reflected a bad habit, a weakness of character. You drank too much you had a hangover. Like that. But wild-card cancer didn't play by his rules. The pancreas? What did he do to deserve that? On November 4 my father's writing stops and someone else is tending to the diary. Her entries are concise: "hospital." "chemotherapy." After a while she settles for the letter "h" to indicate where the old man is. It's as though language itself is failing. On December 11, Else writes the last entry. "Walter ist(um) 4 Uhr von seinen Leiden erlöst worden." At 4 o'clock Walter was released from his suffering. And the word he feared is passed on to me, the heart of my inheritance: never.

IV. The Books of Fritz

Fritz Ensslen, my mother's brother, lived just a mile away from us, worked in the same factory as my father and later, my brother, and along with his wife, my Tante Hede, spent every Friday night of my youth playing pinochle with my parents. I could hear them in the dining room, while I watched Paladin and Gunsmoke in the living room. They drank, they shouted, they slammed cards, my father and Hede against Mom and her brother Fritz, who played quieter hands. The two couples were inseparable. They shopped together, took vacations, celebrated Christmas. Like my father, Fritz had married a German nanny; like my father, he worked as a machinist; but their talents and training differed. Fritz had an artistic bent, his watercolors hang in my house today. Also a socialist, tangling with proto-Nazis in street rumbles, rescued from arrest by another brother who eventually served in the SS. Tall and dark, Fritz must have been a lover too, he left an out-of-wedlock child behind in Germany. Sometime in the 1930's, there'd been talk of bringing Fritzle — little Fritz — to America. Everyone who knows the story is dead but they decided to leave the boy in Germany, with his grandparents. Handsome and wistful as his father, Fritzle died on the Russian front in 1942.

Fritz Ensslen should have been making medical instruments, putting such a skilled tool and die maker on the floor at Wood Newspaper Machinery Co. in Plainfield, New Jersey amounted to assigning a surgeon to operate a meat grinder. Fritz never complained. Among my father and uncles, the loud and hearty crew who gathered at our house on summer Sundays, full of opinions about the Yankees and Joe McCarthy, he stood quietly aside. He ate, drank, sang, danced, but never, it seemed, had much to say. Now I confronted the book he authored, day by day.

They are similar volumes, yearbooks, one for 1952 which served him until 1963, and a 1964 yearbook that ended in 1982. The journal boils the decades down. Fritz was not prolific. He didn't wrestle with feelings, articulate grudges, emote or confide. At the back of the book, neatly printed is a list of purchases and repairs, medical appointments, Christmas card recipients and, at the tail end, the three dates on which his wife was issued speeding tickets, i.e., going 64 in a 55 mile per hour zone on Staten Island, July 18, 1961.

The rest of the book is mostly weather, a daily log of temperature at sunrise and sunset, sunshine and rain. "Hede saw the first five robins," is the first true sentence. Now and then my uncle's careful printing is interrupted by larger, shakier letters: "Fog all day, heavy in the morning," January 15, 1952. I know what is happening, I can picture the scene. At the kitchen in back of the house, where you look out at the rock garden, a hill of flowers, stones, mosses and ceramic elves my uncle periodically repaints, right there in front of the icebox with the radio on top that brings us the Brooklyn Dodgers, right there my cousin Jackie sits in a wheelchair. My uncle holds the book steady with one hand while the other fits a pencil into his son's hands. Jackie was born with infantile paralysis and years later my aunt allowed that the doctors should have "let him go." Still, once he was a part of their lives, they loved him.

Pages of temperature roll past, color coded. At the top corner my uncle summarizes the behavior of particular days: four times, March 16 was clear, three times cloudy, once rainy, once snowy. Birds come and go as spring 1952 rolls in, the first robin on March 13, a fox sparrow on March 22, and my cousin is in and out of the hospital in April and May. No drumrolls, no foregrounding. On July 11: "Jackie don't feel good," and, for the next week, "Jackie still sick," on July 18, "kränky." Anyone can see the end coming; it was never in doubt, not in any of these pieces. But why am I so moved when my uncle Fritz tells me that fifty years ago, on July 21, 1952, the sun rose at 5:42, the sun set at 8:23, at 7 a.m. the temperature was 70 and at 7 p.m. 72 and "Jackie died. 4:50 in Hospital"? A few days later, he lay in the first coffin I'd ever seen, wearing a Brooklyn Dodgers uniform and holding a baseball hat in his hands. Fifty years. I haven't thought about him lately. I don't think that anybody has. Except for me, except for today: I remembered.

In his second book my Uncle Fritz is even more concise: a single line for every day, a circle left un- or half- or fully-shaded, depending on cloud cover. There are highs and lows of temperature, rain and snow. He catches fish in Florida, "3 trouts," and birds appear, finches, first robin, fox sparrow, robin staring next, young purple finches, robin 3 eggs, cuckoo 3 eggs and so his life rolls by, year after year. But not forever. At the end of the book is a graveyard with room for all of us: a list of nearly a hundred names, everyone I ever knew or heard of, a family reunion, some born in 1850, some a hundred years later. Lost grandparents, distant cousins, sweaty hugging tantes, muscular beer-drinking uncles, all there, with the date of their birth, then their death date, followed by a carefully drawn cross. My uncle, my recording angel. First on the list is his brother — my uncle — a Luftwaffe pilot killed in the last weeks of the war. Last on the list is my wife. We're there, the whole bunch, the whole kit and caboodle, and by the time he stopped writing half the names had crosses. When Fritz died in 1987, his widow Hede wrote the date and made a cross. And now I do the same for her: 3/29/98 and — it feels awkward — two lines make a cross.

V. "Freddy Will Want This"

The journals sit on the corner of my desk, waiting to be returned to the file cabinet and it is anybody's guess when, or if, they will be taken out and read again. I don't even want to guess who'll put a date and a cross beside my name. I have been in the company of the dead for around a week and it's hard to say whether I have been visiting them — as my mother would have wished — or they've been visiting me. My father and mother would be a hundred years old next year. If there's a statute of limitations on mourning it has surely passed and anyway, we were a pretty dry-eyed bunch in front of strangers. I cannot weep for them; I'd be weeping for myself. But I miss them, oh how I miss them. Is this permitted, after so long?

Returning from past to present, I glance out at the same campus — Kenyon College — where my mother worried about my happiness. I own a home now and, incredibly, I keep a garden. Mom! I weed, I mulch, I edge! I married and stayed married, true to the saying my brother often quotes: "German Americans are like pumas, they mate for life." I married a woman my mother never met but my father lived to see her a time or two. Five minutes after they were introduced, while we headed to one of the few German restaurants surviving in Manhattan, he took her elbow, slowing their pace while his wife and I proceeded ahead down the sidewalk. He'd tossed and turned for three nights down in Florida when he heard my girlfriend was black. It wasn't as bad as my coming home with a beard, but angst-producing nonetheless. Now, alone with my wife-to-be, he pops the question. "Well," he said. "Do you love him?"

I'm a writer, it's what I do, and there are some things then to see, some books and magazine articles and a couple of movies based on my work. Granted that piece in *Playboy* — "Why They Love Us in the Philippines" — about strip clubs, brothels, foxy-boxing emporia around the Subic Bay Naval Base might have given Mom some pause. And, as for the novels, I'm sure the old man would have urged me to write something more upbeat, more gemütlich, like those old Horatio Hornblower novels. Whatever else he said, I'm sure he'd tell me that no matter whether he disagreed with what I said, he would defend to the death my right to say it.

For a few weeks each summer, this campus fills up with writers — two simultaneous workshops, one for high school kids, one for adults, so there are all kinds of people walking around with notebooks, sitting on front porches, under trees, scribbling during the day, jamming into readings at night. The place is lousy with writers. Looking up from my desk this minute I can see one... no, make it two... writers in the college cemetery, using tombstones as backrests. I've taught in this summer program, I teach fiction workshops in the fall. I talk about voice and pace, time and tone, chronology and closure. I tell people that the point in storytelling is to show, i.e. dramatize, rather than tell. It's the oldest cliche in the business but that doesn't stop it from being true most of the time. Against all these crafty standards and others — breaking experience into scenes, offering a sense of place, identifying significant dramatic transactions — what I took out of the file cabinet falls short. My father's account is choppy and self-centered, my mother's journal way too narrowly focused: the one time she steps off the property and out of the car is November 22, 1963: "What a day. President Kennedy was shot. Hede is in the hospital. Leslie is three." As far as my uncle's nearly hieroglyphic journal of weather, birds and death... well, there's no escaping it, this stuff isn't publishable, it's not literature and there's no way that these things will matter to anyone else as much as they do to me. My relatives weren't interested in entertaining an audience of strangers, which is what I teach my students to do. I ask them to use their lives, their experience, their memories as a point of departure. I invite them to imagine, conjecture, speculate, to take what is true to fiddle with it. The moment always comes when I ask them... require them... to lie in the service of truth. My folks had a different approach. They reduced, they distilled, they boiled down language, narrowed focus, lost the kind of audience they never wanted and drove a stake through my heart. An audience of one. What is, and will be, litter to anyone else is literature to me. At least it does, just barely, what literature is meant to do. It takes the reader to other times and places, it shares secrets and jokes, it confides and hides, links the dead and the living, and for a while anyway, cheats death. My never-fearing father, my worrying-while-weeding mother, my sunrise-sunset recording uncle Fritz — they all live again. Even my so-long-lost cousin: "Jackie died today in the hospital." Well, Jackie dropped in on me this week.

My Private Germany

The Kenyon Review, 2003

Some are in prison, some are dead;
And none has read my books,
And yet my thoughts turn back to them.

from *The Chums* by Theodore Roethke

On a window ledge, above the desk where I grade papers, arrange notes, contend with a phone that does or doesn't ring, there sits a framed black-and-white photo that was taken fifty years ago: my parents, my aunts and uncles on a daytrip from northern New Jersey to Lake Mohonk, in the Catskill Mountains of New York State. Thirteen people, eleven of them German-born, stand on a trail above a lake, a stone cairn and a pine tree just behind them. They are my people, the ones in that picture. They are also my place: where I come from. They're the ones who knew me when I was small, who had hopes for me, and reservations. Now, they watch me work, their scholarship boy, half klutz, half wunderkind. Dead a long time, right on the edge of oblivion, they reproach me. Why haven't I written about them? You're not a kid any more, they remind me. Fair enough. I'm older than they were when our lives touched. I'm nearly as old as they were when they started to die.

There's Pop, always the leader of the pack, standing out in white short-sleeved shirt, slacks held up by suspenders, as close to dressed-up as he ever got. My mother's nearby, smiling, holding up her hand, maybe to wave at the camera, maybe to shade her eyes. Was I the photographer? I was along that day in the Catskills but I'm not in the photo. "You were always someplace else, wandering around," my Tante Hede told me, when I asked her years later. She was my last link to the family past. She remembered holding my mother in her arms, both sobbing, listening to the screams coming from inside the doctor's office where I was being circumcised. Now she is someplace else too, her ashes scattered around a sycamore tree in our old neighborhood. Walter, Hans, Fritz, Rupert, John, Carrie, Paula, Else, Hede, Maria, Friedel, on the edge of time and memory, except for the stay of execution my words provide. American citizens, New Jersey residents. Residents, as well, of a dogged land which I've spent all my life trying to take the measure of, in them, in me: my private Germany.

"My Parents Before I Knew Them." In my family, I am the custodian of albums, loose photographs, diaries, letters, expired passports, birth and death certificates, all sorts of souvenirs and keepsakes. "My Parents Before I Knew Them" is an album I put together of family photographs taken before my birth in 1942. Mom and Pop were both 39 when I was born and I missed knowing them when they were young, during their "greenhorn" years in America. I missed a lot. So there is my father, a boy swimming in the Elbe, behind him ships at anchor. And my mother looking melancholy beneath a blossoming Swabian apple tree, homesick even before leaving Germany. And, further back in time, there are whole generations — a grandfather in a spiked World War I helmet, a great-uncle with an iron cross from the Franco-Prussian war, a great aunt who became Mayor of Berlin. There are my grandfathers, a Hamburg coppersmith, a furniture maker in Stuttgart. South Germans and North Germans, wine drinkers versus beer drinkers, potato eaters versus noodle makers, converging on New Jersey, and in me. My mother came first, in 1922. In those days German nannies were still in demand by wealthy New Yorkers and there she is, just out of Ellis Island — she remembered the cockroaches — living near where Zabar's is today, wheeling somebody's baby in Riverside Park. Served corn-on-the-cob for the first time, she bit straight into it as if it were a bratwurst. For my father, America's first magic was the oranges for sale on the streets of New York. No wonder, at the end of his life, he found his way to Florida. During the war and the British blockade, he'd subsisted on turnips. After he came to America, he never ate another turnip. My father was sponsored by the legendary Uncle Bruno, who brought over one greenhorn at a time, half a dozen at least, giving them brief employment as a janitor in a building where he was superintendent, at 125th Street and Seventh Avenue. My father slept in the basement, on a cot next to the boiler and, during his first days, couldn't resist picking things out of the garbage that came down the dumbwaiter, ladies shoes with weeks of wear left in them, perfect for his sister back in Hamburg.

They met, I'm told, at a German picnic in Jersey City. The engagement celebration was at a Horn and Hardart's automat. They were a couple now, the bandy-legged, barrel-chested machinist and the quiet, thoughtful housewife. They did not linger in New York, not even in the German-American enclave of Yorkville, with its beer halls, bakeries and oom-pah-pah. They moved to Miami — married there in 1926 — back to New York, to Philadelphia, then to New Jersey, twenty miles west of the Holland Tunnel, "out in the sticks." They were finishing up a house there when World War II began and I was born, started to know and to wonder.

Start with my first memory, those long brown rolls of wrapping paper just inside the side door of our house, on the steps leading up to the kitchen, those assembly lines of neighborhood tantes joining my mother in expertly jamming soap, toothpaste, razor blades, coffee, Crisco, into five-pound "Germany packages" headed for bombed-out relatives who were — no double entendre intended — "on the other side." They took the packages to shipping firms in Yorkville, they drove to Philadelphia when the surrendered German pocket battleship Prinz Eugen arrived on its way to nuclear tests in the Marshall Islands and word came that the German crew was willing to carry packages back across the Atlantic. In Germany, a New Jerseyan in the occupying forces befriended a tante living outside Stuttgart and agreed to pass along packages addressed to him. He was a guest at New Jersey beer parties for years afterward. "We spent thousands and thousands of dollars on those packages," the neighbor Tante told me years later, when we were both back in Germany. She paused a moment, looked outside the kitchen we were sitting in, out onto the cobblestoned streets, freshly plastered buildings, tidy gardens of a prosperous post-war Germany. "They wouldn't have done the same for us," she said. In private moments, they must all have wondered what gifts would have come their way, if Adolf had won.

What we got back were the "Deutschland pakete" that arrived at Christmas, when I sensed our Germanness the most. Our celebration was all on Christmas Eve — Americans waited till after breakfast to open presents. My presents were history by then. We gathered at dusk, my parents, the onkels and tantes, beginning at our house, moving on to two or three others. We sang "Silent Night" in German. That was mandatory for kids. And the first gifts we opened were the ones from the other side. They didn't amount to much. Crinkly paper decorated with sprigs of pine, the needles long since fallen off. A necktie my father would never wear, some marzipan for me, some schnappsbohnen — whiskey-filled pralines — that had usually melted en-route. An odd little ceremony before the unwrapping of the big ticket items began, a moment of silence for a hated nation where there were people my parents loved.

I wondered about the war years. My parents were loyal Americans, I was sure of that. My father had worked in a factory that shifted from locomotives to tanks. He'd shrugged off invitations to a pre-war German-American Bund camp. Later, when asked whether German Field Marshal Hans Gunter Von Kluge was a relative, he fired back, "Oh yeah, that's my uncle." And returned to work on tanks. My mother and aunt got dirty looks when they spoke German while shopping. Piddling stuff. But there must have been darker moments that I was too young to notice. How did they feel watching newsreels, hundreds of planes bombing their home cities? The world applauding while their relatives died? What about those slow-coming letters, routed through Switzerland, telling them that one of my uncles had been killed on the Russian front? "In Russland gefallen." I grew up wondering about the people on the other side. Were there any good ones? No heroes. The South had heroes in the Civil War. But not the Germans? Was there no one to mourn? I remember a rainy afternoon my mother and I spent sitting on the floor of my room, sorting through a box of loose photographs — trips to Florida, the building of our house, my brother's Boy Scout camping trips — and then she was holding a picture of a handsome, sharp-featured fellow in a Luftwaffe uniform. She fell silent. My mother was thoughtful and reticent: the emotions she expressed were thrice-distilled. "That's your uncle Paul," she told me after a while. He'd died just two weeks before the war in Europe ended, while riding in a hospital train that had been strafed. He was her favorite brother and she mourned for him. "He was the best of us all," she said.

My mother saw her favorite brother for the last time in 1936. A photo of that trip sat in the living room: my mother, smiling, surrounded by three brothers and a nephew, all of them in uniform: Paul in Hitler Youth, Fritzle — later killed in Russia — and Walter in Wehrmacht uniforms, and Willi in the ominous black of the SS, a swastika armband above his elbow. I studied that picture for years. It fascinated me knowing that uncles of mine, beloved of my mother, could be part of something evil. It complicated my view of good, of evil, of heroes and villains, of war movies with monocled fascist officers, chuckling U-boat captains, hapless sentries quickly stabbed and garroted. I developed what I've never lost: an interest in the other side.

For sure, we were Americans in the New Jersey of the fifties. My mother cooked and gardened. She ate a piece of chocolate and read an article in *Reader's Digest* every night, and when she worried, it wasn't about war and loyalty. It was about me. School counselors had called her in and told her that I was something called "college material."

She spent a lot of time wondering where that would lead. Outgoing, opinionated, physical, my father worried not at all. I picture him on Sundays, wearing shorts and, underneath the shorts, a pair of boxer underwear that always were an inch or so longer than the shorts. I see him in the yard, sweating and bare-chested, waving cheerfully to well-dressed church-goers then, when he finished working, sitting on the front stoop with a Ballantine Ale. He was an American success story by then. They all were, and I think of them as happy in America. He took me on camping trips, organized Boy Scout newspaper drives, paid union dues, voted Democrat, never missed the beautiful music on "The Voice of Firestone." On vacations they went to Florida or went west to national parks, always traveling with tantes and onkels, recording mileage, meals and gas prices along the way and never registering in a motel room until sending one of the women inside, to make sure the place was clean.

Still, Germany remained, for them and for me. It was in the language we spoke at home, so that I went to school with a German accent that caught the attention of a speech therapist: "washing machine, washing machine, washing machine," I was made to repeat. It was in the food — the roast pork with skin on, potato pancakes, herring salad, rouladen — unfashionable food that I'll never taste again. It was in the loud, smokey table-banging pinochle they played every weekday night for thirty years, hoots and gibes that roared into the living room where I sat watching *Paladin* and *Gunsmoke*. They played for money that no one won. Losers contributed to a savings account — a sparkasse — that financed the next trip back to Germany. But I never felt more German-in-New

Jersey than at the beer parties we had in the summer. I still hear the crunch of cars coming down the driveway, onkels and tantes pulling in from New York and Long Island, carrying cakes and cold cuts they'd picked up in the city. In the afternoon it was cake and coffee, it was garden walks and sitting in lawn chairs, American success stories posing in front of turkeys for pictures they'd send to the other side. As darkness rolled on, things got loud and a little rowdy. They drank beer, they sang old songs — German songs, some homesick, some political — and when they decided to dance, an onkel pulled out an accordion and they adjourned inside our garage and those were the sounds I heard from where I was upstairs sleeping, drowsy from the beer they'd given me. Those were my lullabies.

In 1954, the poker-losings added up: we were going back to Germany, my parents, three sets of aunts and uncles and a great aunt who'd known Lou Gehrig's parents when they were neighbors up on Amsterdam Avenue. "Lou was a nice boy," she said. There was another man, Hans, a German Jew whom members of a Tante's family had concealed in their cellar during the war. I was the "Kleine Amerikaner," the precocious diary-keeper:

> We all said that we would not cry when we arrived in Stuttgart. Well, there is where we made a mistake. We all cried, except Pop as far as I could see. Most everybody I had ever heard of in letters was there and there were still some left over. I have never seen so much pure joy before and probably never will again. After that, we went to a hall where we could be together for a while. I got a model ship from Tante Martha, the toy shop owner in Winnenden. It was very nice. I really like everyone. We

> slept at Onkel Walter's. When we were in Rotterdam, Tante Helen threw up from seasickness even though she was no longer at sea.

Two of the uncles I studied for years were waiting for us at the Stuttgart station. Walter was a tall genial man, a furniture maker — that was the family trade — who gave me chores in his shop, sweeping up wood scraps and sawdust. He'd been in the Army, in ski troops, and had slipped out of a P.O.W. camp and found his way home. By 1954, Willi — the SS lieutenant — was a sweaty, high-strung corpulent man, an endlessly busy host, planning trips and meals a week ahead, meals in, meals out, big and little, hot and cold. He was one of those Germans who came out of the war eating and never stopped. Still, there were remnants of the kind of masculine handsomeness you don't see anymore: the dark, straight black hair, the heavy beard, the roustabout adventurousness of a Clark Gable or Ernest Hemingway, a Jack Dempsey or Max Schmeling. In a firmly Socialist family, he'd rebelled and joined the Nazi party early. Yet he was there for his socialist brothers, intervening in their behalf when they got in trouble with the new regime. It was always Willi to the rescue, I was told. The stories were impossible to sort out. He'd refused to participate in a firing squad. He had not joined the party to kill Jews he said, and these were Jews from Stuttgart. His insubordination landed him in a punishment battalion — strafsbattalion — on the Russian front, where he was gravely wounded, shrapnel that he carried in his head for the rest of his life. It was after this wound or possibly an earlier one, that Hitler, visiting a hospital, gave birth to my best one-degree of separation story: the Fuhrer chucked him under the chin affectionately. In 1945, Willi was in Berlin, swarming with

Russians and — the story was — he shed his uniform, put on a civilian suit and made his way through the lines carrying a wreath of flowers, pretending he was on his way to his grandmother's funeral. "Babushka kaput," he told the Russians. The Americans came for him once he was home, held him for a couple of years until he was cleared, supposedly by the testimony of one of the Jews he'd spared. Were these stories my parents made up to tell me? That he made up to tell them? That he told himself? I'll never know. I can only consider the possibilities, which is what my private Germany is all about, the chance of good, of evil, of both, then and now, in them, in me. Possibilities from here to the airport, the currency of the realm.

From 1954, I remember the taste of hard cider, the coarseness of toilet paper, the whiff of fresh bread at dawn, wafting out of bakeries onto cobblestone streets. We visited all three of Ludwig's Bavarian castles, drove across the Alps down to Venice, my uncle wisecracking about the slovenly performance of the Duce's troops in World War II, the same jokes that circulated in New Jersey's public high schools: "Want to buy a rifle that was owned by an Italian war hero? Never been fired, only dropped once." That was it: history into stories, jokes, and silence.

I wonder how we looked to them, we German-Americans who sent back pictures of the turkeys we ate at Thanksgiving, the cars we drove to Florida. I wonder what they thought of me, the chubby baseball fan who spoke broken German. I wonder, as with all reunions, which prevailed, the feeling of distance or connection. They never talked about the war, not when I was around and, I'd bet, not when I wasn't. No talk of politics or principles, no finding of fault, no measuring of private virtue and public crime. That's one vote for distance. But there were moments when we drove down bombed-out streets, there were pauses when they talked about the dead. There was the look on my mother's face when we visited the Luftwaffe pilot's grave, the date of his death just a couple of weeks before the end of the war in Europe. In that, in the unspoken love and pole-axed silence, there was a recognition that what had happened to them could have happened to us. We were family. One vote for connection.

If you grow up in New Jersey and have a knack for words, New York City is your Oz. Driving along wooded roads in the Watchung Mountains, parking in secluded cul de sacs on high school dates, I'd see that river of traffic down on Route 22, headed for the tunnel, that carpet of lights spread out below, shopping centers, factories, endless suburbs, my New Jersey alive and pungent, just stinking with promise. And, in the distance, the towers of Manhattan, where the future waited. And the past. When I moved there in 1970 to work for *Life* magazine, I was drawn to the old German neighborhood of Yorkville. I strolled 86th Street, where Germans once drank beer and danced. When I jogged around the northern end of Central Park, I nodded at the building where my father had slept in the basement, his first night in America. In Riverside Park, watching the sun set over New Jersey's richly polluted skies, I imagined my mother pushing a baby carriage along these very paths, meeting up with other nannies sitting on this same bench. I felt close to them, sometimes. On Broadway, there was a barbershop, one of the last that offered shaves. The barbers were Italians of my father's generation, skillful and reserved.

Stretched out in a chair, my face covered with a hot towel, I'd glance up at a stamped tin ceiling, a slowly turning fan. A baseball game was on the radio. Your world, Pop, I said to myself. Even as it was all slipping away.

"There goes another one," they used to say when they got a bad news phone call, when a Christmas or two passed without a card arriving. My mother was the first to go, laconic and heart-felt in her final words to me. With a friend waiting in the driveway, my ride back to graduate school at the University of Chicago, I ducked into her bedroom to say goodbye. She cried, whenever we parted. "See," she said to me, holding back her tears. "I've finally learned to say goodbye." The next minute I was gone and a month later so was she. My father never forgave her for ruining one last trip out west, one last trip to Germany. Before long, they all were making terminal moves. "This one will last me out," they said when they bought new cars. Unable to pay suburban property taxes after they stopped working, they moved to retirement communities in South Jersey, in the Pine Barrens near Lakewood, within jogging distance of the place where the Hindenburg had crashed. My father flirted with going back to Hamburg, of sitting in a beer garden above the Elbe, watching ships sail in from around the world. It appealed to him, being old where he'd been young. But in the end, Florida won: today's oranges over yesterday's turnips. I was halfway around the world when he died. So I have no last words. My brother was there at the end. Seeing my father in pain, he asked whether "You want a shot, Pop?" "Yes," Pop said, "I'd like a shot." But it came in a syringe, not in the whiskey glass he'd wanted.

Before long, my private Germany was hard to find. It wasn't in New Jersey, it wasn't in Germany. And certainly not in New York. The Germans didn't stick around the old neighborhood and once they were gone, their businesses were replaced by Irish bars, Korean fruit stands, discount clothing stores and running shoe shops. You could see it in the parades on Fifth Avenue. St. Patrick's Day was raucous and hard-drinking, Puerto Rican parades bristled with horn-blowing machismo, the State of Israel celebration with pride and clout. The German Von Steuben parade was an orderly procession that disbanded on 86th Street in a neighborhood that no longer existed. Manhattan had more Ethiopian restaurants than German. It was over, almost everywhere. Except in me.

I could feel it, as the years passed. My old man was punctual. Dinner on the table at six o'clock sharp. If someone invited us for 8:30, Pop was on the doorstep on the dot, even if the host came to the door in a bathrobe. I'm like that now, too. And I share his obsession with work done on time, always a little bit extra, even if people laugh at you. I feel his admiration for smarts even if out of shyness, arrogance, whatever… I sense that some kinds of cleverness are not for me. I concur that a bill left unpaid, sitting on a table overnight, is as troubling as an un-pulled weed in a garden and — this from my mother — that the morning after a rainy day is a perfect day for weeding. I garden more than I ever dreamed, listen to more opera, believe that any large withdrawal from my savings account is the first step leading to death in the gutter. And I can't bring myself to throw out an article of clothing that has "wear" left in it, however soiled and out of fashion it might be. And, incredibly, I'm neater. "Ein Platz Für Alles, und Alles in Sein Platz" — a place for everything and everything in its place. The kid who spent years trying to convince his parents that messy was not the same as dirty, that kid puts his clothes away now! There are more serious things too. There's that inbred feeling for the other side, even though the other side — my father in this case — didn't support me. His commitment to the United States was firm. When I had my doubts about Viet Nam, he treated me as if I were shirking garden work. "You think you can pick your wars?" he asked. That was the point exactly, I said, and Germans of all people should have learned by now. He wasn't impressed. Still, my private Germany resurged during the seventies, that interest in the other side. In my darkest moods, I pictured a war crimes trial, America's first taste of victor's justice. I didn't want to see it, mind you, but I had to wonder. I'd read endlessly about Nuremberg. How would Americans acquit themselves? Was Robert McNamara our Albert Speer, Westmoreland our Keitel? Who would feign madness like Hess? Discover religion, like Hans Frank? Who, like Goering, would bait and ridicule, knowing he had a capsule of cyanide hidden in his rectum? I couldn't help it. Being American, yet resident of a private Germany, meant that winners and losers, heroes and villains connected in me. I had ties to a nation that had known spectacular defeat and that gave me an edge on America in the seventies. Germans, in their awkward way, were ahead of Americans. Germans knew, Germans learned that good men do bad. That lives are lost for nothing. In school I'd been taught that America never started a war. That was lesson one. And never lost a war. Lesson two. In Germany, wars were started and lost. And everyone with some German in them had traveled to a place no American had ever been, way out on the last frontier: defeat.

On the afternoon of my fortieth high school reunion, I head home. I turn the car I rented at Newark Airport down the street I know by heart, past where we waited for the school bus, past the neighbor's house and I slow, I stop, looking in at where I lived. My private Germany, an American place in the last analysis. A miracle of love for America, of abiding concern for the people on the other side. They pulled it off quietly, cheerfully. They made less of it than I have. Two owners since the old man sold, but the trees he planted on weekends tower over the tiny house. I see the stoop where he drank his Ballantine Ale, the chicken coop out back, my bedroom window. The place is still there — the landscape of spruce and maples, the gravel driveway, the remnant gardens. It's the kind of golden-rich autumn afternoon that conduces to memory, that invites nostalgia. But no one's home. An empty stage inside an empty theater. The houses outlasted us all, the onkels and tantes, the people who built, sold, traded up, moved out into America. I've been missing them for years, that bunch, resenting every intervening day that separated them from me, leaving me to wonder about a chess set that Willi carved after the war while the Americans held him in Dachau; a dress sword with a swastika that belonged to Paul; a beer stein with socialist heroes, from Spartacus to Liebknecht, to Marx and Engels, a kind of Miller Time in left-wing heaven, courtesy of my father's father; a collection of letters, yellow and crumbling; logs from long-ago trips to Florida; diaries that end in death. And that reproaching photo across my desk — all these things with no one to claim them, after me. And yet, I was stopped cold by that remark in Bellow's *Ravelstein* that, no matter what we say we think, despite all our tough talk, a part of us believes that we will someday talk with our parents again. Sometimes it feels that they are still out there with their short-sleeved shirts and their big American cars, their small houses and spectacular gardens, waiting for me. "Sit on the table... eat your plate," they tell their kids at dinnertime. Rooting for the Brooklyn Dodgers, laughing at Jackie Gleason, and waiting for me. And my aunt was right, I was always someplace, always wandering off. For years they were drifting away from me, further into the past, the way an island sinks beneath the horizon. But now I feel time rounding, I feel myself coming closer to them, a reunion imminent in my private Germany and many conversations we never got to have, along with beer and cake and the smell of cut grass and drowsy with Ballantine beer, I will fall asleep in my house, my room, hearing the songs of the other side as they escape into no man's land from time's dug-in trenches and go sailing out into the New Jersey evening.

Day By Day

Kenyon College Alumni Bulletin, Winter 2016

I can't help wondering about my life in Gambier, about what captured and kept me here. Late summer evenings on a succulently empty campus conduce this kind of reflection. I sit on a chair in back of my house, a place that was once a dormitory, ordered up by Philander Chase in 1827, later moved to the site of the Kenyon Inn and then to its current location on Ward Street. This house has outlasted a lot of careers; I'm not its first occupant nor its last. The house, like the College, is a place we pass through. Houses have no memories, nor do institutions. People do, though.

And that returns to the question: Why Gambier? Was the decision to stay about integrity? Compromise? It could go either way. But then, while mulling this over, I can hear cows lowing in nearby fields, and, coming from another direction, the bells pealing in the Church of the Holy Spirt; and I can't help feeling that I am where I ought to be.

I am about a three-minute walk from Lewis Hall, my freshman dorm. The place has a certain smell — cleaning fluid, floor wax, dirty laundry, sweat, pizza and testosterone. Spray a whiff of it under my nose on the last day of my life, and I would know it.

Later, I spent two years as a resident in nearby Norton Hall. That was a time when I stayed up all night, reading until dawn. Someone was always awake, wandering the halls, chatting about nothing in particular in the lounge. "Pulling an all-nighter" — like "going to the library" — didn't necessarily require studying. It was as though we were shipwrecked: 500 males and 40 faculty members marooned on this hill. The distances were longer then, the nights were darker. In spite of all that, maybe because of it, the place had an eccentric magic.

Every walk I take here these days is on memory lane. I step into Peirce Hall, though it is not permitted to pass through the doors that once led us into that awesome stain-glassed, portrait-bedecked, dark wood room where I remember Smokey Robinson and The Miracles performing "Tracks of My Tears" in front of the high table. Afterward, I induced Ronnie White, co-founder of the group, to a party at the Psi U Lounge in North Leonard. I can't forget his puzzlement, glancing around a room that was almost entirely male. "What do you guys do here?" Words failed me at the time. A dateless life. But did it make sense to transfer because you couldn't get a date here?

On another dateless weekend, a dance weekend, I meandered downhill to where a bridge — since destroyed — spanned the Kokosing River near Laymon Road. This was the setting for an early-morning gathering of the hungover, the dateless and bird-dogged, who assembled to elect "the asshole of the year." Bridge and party are history now.

People return and press me for my opinions about Kenyon. Sometimes they're looking for a booster. Sometimes they're looking for somebody a bit cranky. Has it changed? For the better? Is every decision prudent and wise? I'm asked to reach into my bag of nostalgia, appreciation, reservation and outright dismay. There's a lot to care about and a lot to worry about.

One thing I'll give anybody: There are always good reasons to leave Gambier. Love it and leave it. It's a company town after all, and you need to distance yourself. Funny thing though, I start missing the place almost instantly. In Singapore, Palau, Malacca, Sydney, Vienna, I start musing about Gambier. I like my life here.

My 24 hours in Gambier isn't like it was when I was a student. Students, as ever, stay up until the wee hours — one a.m. is early to bed for them. The dorms are an alternate universe, located in another time zone. Breakfast is a land they never visit.

But for me, Gambier is a morning place: At dawn I have my first coffee at home, checking to see what predators — groundhogs, deer, raccoons, skunks — have turned my garden into a salad bar. Then I sit around Wiggin Street Café, where people drop by, a kind of cabal that mulls over sports; master plans; hirings; firings; funerals; trees cut, fallen, planted; ups and downs of administration. After that, if there's time, I drive downhill, turn right onto 229, continue about 100 yards and turn uphill to the Franklin Miller Observatory, find a bench, and I'm surrounded by woodlots, fences, grazing cows. This is a place that concentrates thought and calms feelings. There's nothing in view that's ugly. It can be hard to find a place like this.

By mid-morning I am in my office, door ajar. I encourage students to visit at any time, but there's not much morning traffic. *The New York Times* crossword puzzle requires me to pick up a pen and keep it there. After the puzzle is done, lecture notes, student papers (shift to red ink) and my own scribbling. In the early afternoon I enter the Kenyon Athletic Center. I worried about its cost and its hangar-like appearance. But I'm hooked. Some afternoons I arrange a trip to Mount Vernon on this or that errand. The journey, not the destination, is what matters. I meander down Lower Gambier Road — a.k.a. River Road. Live here, your interest in the river is proprietary. You watch it go from gentle to raging wild, flooding adjoining corn and soy fields, those same fields that sprout seedlings when our students graduate, then are brown, broken stubble a bit after the first-year kids settle in. Across the river, I glimpse the most likable change I've seen: a running trail, once a railroad track, that runs 13 miles from Mount Vernon to Danville, cutting through ferny, shaded forests, pungent cow pastures, and marshland where frogs and turtles plop off logs and lily pads as you pass. I've covered every inch of that trail though not, I have to add, all in one run.

And now: teaching, professing, my work. I've become nocturnal. I prefer the night shift, evening seminars that go from 7 to 10 p.m. These sessions, I suspect, may go the way of Sunday doubleheaders. I confront students, putting their creative writing talent — and ego — at stake on a seminar table. I admire them for taking a chance on fiction. I also warn them that the world isn't necessarily waiting for their sunrise. It's the kind of seminar that people take personally — ask John Green or Ransom Riggs. I take it personally as well.

After class, I can't just go to bed at 10 p.m. Whether it went well or less well, I mull it over. I have a drink. I watch something mindless on television — at these times, the Shopping Channel will do. I have evening office hours as well. Sometimes, I'm left to enjoy my own company. Other times, I'm busier than a union dentist. Either way, it's strange. Once I was a student whose day was made if Denham Sutcliffe tossed me a line as I passed his office, wondering if he had read my paper. Now, I'm the one in the office, waiting for someone to come by. Maybe a younger version of myself. Then again, even on slow nights, I'm tipping my hat in the direction of a man — dead more than half a century — who meant a lot to me.

In 1991-92, while reporting *Alma Mater,* a nonfiction account of a year in the life of Kenyon College, I moved back into Lewis Hall. For this alone, I deserved serious Nobel Prize consideration. I kept a distance from the inmates at first, but by the end of that year I knew them well. Some are still in touch. Others, I have wondered about. And this year, as at previous reunions, some stay at my house, corning home at anywhere between 1 and 4 a.m. Like an anxious parent, I listen for these 42-year-olds' footsteps.

And it's all about memory, personal and shared. Students recall things I said in class, dispensed on their papers. One student confided that he'd been guided for years by something I told him, something that had gotten him through some rough spots. I had no idea what I was in for. "You told me," he said, "that everybody is somebody's asshole." That may not quite be what Henry Adams had in mind when he remarked, "A teacher affects eternity; he can never tell where his influence stops." You bet.

That's it. It's about keeping in touch with the past, sharing the present, and confronting whatever the future bequeaths. There are many colleges, surely as fine, possibly finer. It doesn't matter. I will leave her again and again, for good reason. But I will return. And at the end, my returns will outnumber, by one, my departures.

Travel Writing

I'm a traveler. But my kind of travel requires a serious commitment. I don't believe in single visits to "bucket list" destinations. One trip isn't enough: one is not done. One trip is shallow, negligible. I espouse repeat visits. Consider Altaussee, Austria in the lake and mountain district south of Salzburg. We've visited at least a dozen times, two or three weeks each. As we grow older, our sojourns grow longer. We're not voters, citizens, landowners, taxpayers; but neither are we tourists. We revisit my Peace Corps islands of Saipan and Palau. We return again and again to Singapore, Malacca, Manila. We can't avoid Mount Wilson in the Blue Mountains of Australia. Granted, there's a daunting list of places we'll never see. But we cherish places we visit repeatedly. Places that keep on generating memories. And memories are keepers. A few years ago, on my umpteenth return to Palau, a local newspaper published a photo and a short story — KLUGE VISITS AGAIN the headline proclaimed. That says it all.

Return to Paradise

National Geographic Traveler, Oct 2002, Volume 19 No. 7

The odds are long, I admit, but I return to Bali to correct a mistake, to find what may be lost forever. In 1977, in a small gallery in the village of Ubud, I saw a painting that tempted me. Picture a Hindu temple in a forest clearing lit by a full moon. In an eerie union of the animal and the spiritual, three monkeys are perched upon a temple pillar, embracing stone gods, seeming to both blaspheme and worship at once. For whatever reason — shipping, money — I passed the painting by, a bad decision that haunts me even now. I have no idea whether the painting is great art, the product of an individual talent, or a village assembly line as common as big-eyed puppies. But I want it.

There was a lot of Bali in that painting. Beyond the celebrated surf and beaches, the rice terraces and volcanoes and, nowadays, beyond the white-water rafting, bungee jumping, and swimming with dolphins — the island has a spiritual depth, a version of Hinduism that defines and orders life at every level, creating a tight weave of ritual and offering. The spectacle of belief, the spell of magic, that's Bali. It's not just a painting that I'm looking for, I realize. It is Bali itself.

Bali is the quintessential paradise, "the morning of the world," in the words of Indian leader Jawaharlal Nehru. When I return to Bali, however, it feels a little later in the day. An hour inland from the airport, Ubud is unrecognizable. The island of gods now has cappuccino and Internet cafes, wall-to-wall art galleries, souvenir shops, restaurants, and money changers. Idling drivers offer to transport me; sidewalk touts peddle tickets for that night's dance performances. "The place has become a destination for culture vultures," one longtime resident later tells me. A Balinese businessman agrees. "All over the world people know Bali. And all over Indonesia people know that Bali is a very good place to earn money."

I go looking for a dirt path that once led from the center of town out into the rice fields, ending at the monkey forest sanctuary with a temple at its center. The path, I discover, is now Monkey Forest Road, paved and lined with tourist shops. It's late afternoon when I reach the forest. Tourists are posing their kids with the monkeys. At the temple, a monkey climbs up a pillar, turning my painting's haunting tableau into a snapshot.

So, it seems, time has not been kind, that's all. In the words of local writer and landscape architect Made Wijaya, Bali has been transformed from a "user-friendly magic kingdom into a high-density paradise theme park." I wonder what it will take to turn my trip around, to find the magic. Then I calm down. I slow down. I stop worrying. I almost stop moving. I talk to people. And bit by bit, the magic finds me.

"Back in the '70s I was stressed out of my mind," says the man I'm staying with, a friend of a friend. "I was starting to twitch. To recover, I was told I had to go somewhere for at least three weeks where there was no telephone." He came to Bali, stayed briefly in crowded Kuta, then decided to head for the hills. "I walked out into the villages," he recalls. "I watched lizards stalk flies. I watched bamboo grow. I reconnected with life. I found an amazing house and view.

And then it was like a door inside myself opened — and I walked through it." The place my friend came to and made his home is a small sliver of land overlooking a terraced hillside of rice paddies. Far down from the edge of the property, the Ayung River flows. During the day, kids swim there. At night, in season, fireflies flicker. Host and guests share meals at an open-air dining pavilion, then retire to thatch-roofed cottages. Sleeping out on the porch, under a mosquito net, I'm as excited as a kid camping in a pup tent on the lawn. I hear cicadas, toads, and geckos, a nightly battle of the bands a few feet from my pillow. I hear the river and, some nights, the sound of rain coursing off the roof, falling onto broad-leaved plants, dripping further into lily ponds.

But moonlit nights are best. As the moon rises, it gilds the river below us, and later, it tints the fog that rolls in over the rice paddies. Moonlight in Bali conduces to magic, combining the best of light and dark, suggesting possibilities. It reminds me of that painting I may never find. Mornings begin with roosters crowing, ducks quacking sardonically, grouchy dogs getting into arguments. Houseboys put out offerings to the gods, delicate arrangements of rice and flowers deposited at different locations around this small property.

The rice terraces are the first things I look at in the morning. Granted, to openly admire rice paddies is to label yourself a hopeless tourist. Well, call me a tourist, but all around Ubud are memorable scenes: temples and shrines right among the rice, endless conjugations of the color green, subtle arrangements of land and water. The same rice farmers I see working at dawn and dusk may be found later playing in temple gamelan orchestras that send their pounding homegrown Indonesian music across the paddies late at night. In the distance stand volcanoes, warning that angry gods might yet be heard from.

I take my host's advice. I head for the hills, the villages, to search for my lost painting, not the very same painting — I know better than to hope for that — but the same scene, the same mood and magic. There's hope. In Bali, the arts are folk arts, and part of the folk art tradition is imitation.

"It appears that each Balinese native from the womb to the tomb is creative," rhymed Noël Coward on a 1930s tour of Bali. It's still that way. In Tegallalang, everyone seems to have been life-sentenced to high school wood shop. Sidewalks are covered with carved cats, buffalo, egrets. One hamlet specializes in fish mobiles, another in birds. In Celuk it's silver; in Mas, masks; in Sukuwati, gold and silver umbrellas. Yet my painting eludes me. I go to museums, galleries, and studios, interrogating proprietors, describing what I seek — and getting shrugs. I find paintings with village scenes, temple scenes, scenes out of Hindu epics, wizened farms and winsome women, horses, flowers, ghosts, lovers. The sheer volume gets numbing. Paintings that start out lively soon seem busy, overdecorated, and it doesn't help when, admiring one work, you find a dozen similar ones up and down the street. Sometimes I wonder what I would do if I managed to come across my painting again. Would I still like it?

To the Balinese, seeing beauty, no matter what type, "washes the eyes," cleansing away the day's dust and grit, the imperfections and disappointments. My painting may be a lost cause, but not the search for it, for I see beauty at every turn. Going through a Balinese village in late afternoon washes my eyes. I see men relaxing in front of roadside stores. In stately processions, women step out of side alleys and walk along the road, carrying piles of fruit on their heads, offerings for the temple. Ducks get shepherded through traffic; kids splash in streams that burst out of fern-covered hillsides. A temple chant calls people to worship.

I'm in a taxi headed from Ubud to Denpasar, Bali's provincial capital, to keep an appointment with Degung Santikarma, a writer and anthropologist whose comments on tourism caught my eye. "Although I am Balinese, I am not an artist or dancer," he has written. "I am not a gamelan addict, either. I am a man who loves the Colonel from Kentucky."

Good-humored and sharp-tongued, Santikarma had suggested over lunch that the Bali that tourists see is a kind of theater catering to "Western stereotypes of spiritual, nature-loving, and peaceful Balinese." The island's history is more complicated than that, Santikarma knows. His father and uncles were executed in the violence that swept Indonesia in 1965. The present day is also tricky, with concerns about immigration, pollution, crowding, debates about outsider-owned resort hotels, golf courses that soak up island water like sponges. Are the Balinese getting too little money from tourism? Too much? "Sometimes we're the victims," Santikarma claims. "Sometimes we're the agents." Approaching the center of Denpasar, I abandon the taxi when the streets get clogged. I pass a crowded cockfight arena, go up and down some steps which take me into a densely packed temple compound, where Santikarma is waiting for me. The air is heavy with imminent rain, drenched with smoke and incense, charged up by gamelan music. A half dozen pavilions are piled high with offerings, and people are standing, sitting, kneeling on the ground in prayer and, it seems, waiting for something to happen.

Then, without warning, there comes a harrowing scream. Ten feet away a young man is having a fit. Eyes rolling, arms and legs flailing, he's in the grip of something. Three friends restrain him when he goes into motion, prop him up when he goes limp. They guide him to the center of the pavilion. Now there are similar outbreaks throughout the crowd, a couple dozen of them, all dragged into a procession, which exits the temple and circles the nearby cockpit for an hour. At one moment, the trance dancers are spent and helpless. Then, the gamelan music stirs them, the spirit resurges, and they are wild-eyed and whooping. They return to the temple spent, sweating, sometimes drooling. Later, Santikarma tells me, the trance dancers have little memory of what happened or what led them to it. This wasn't just a performance for tourists, I conclude. The dancers were playing to a higher audience: their gods. Leaving the temple with Santikarma, walking through a crowded night market, I ask what he makes of this annual temple celebration. "I like it," he quietly allows.

At a party in Ubud I hear a story: A tourist ship calls at a small island in the Nusa Tenggara group east of Bali. "Do not buy the caged birds for sale on shore," warns the onboard lecturer. "Do not encourage such a pernicious trade." All the tourists obey, except for one elderly lady who takes pity on a bird that has a broken leg. If she doesn't buy the bird, she reasons, it will surely die. What becomes of the bird or the lady is unknown. But the next year the same ship calls at the same island, and the same selling of birds occurs, with a difference: This time all the birds have broken legs.

The story, whether or not it actually happened, makes me shudder. Indeed, bad things can result when the world visits an island, and Bali is no exception. Two reactions to this long-worried-over paradise occur almost simultaneously: "Eureka, I've found it!" and "It isn't what it used to be."

Both are valid. Bali is more crowded than before, yet its religiously-based sense of self is still formidable and its looks are still heart stopping — the rice terraces and villages, the temples, and near the end of my stay, the Seniwati Gallery in Ubud. The place was founded by Mary Northmore, an Englishwoman who married an Indonesian artist. When she asked around about the dearth of local women painters, she was told it was because "Balinese women have no sense of color." Her rejoinder is the Seniwati Gallery, dedicated to art by women.

On my first visit, I'm pleased by an intricate landscape of trees and paddies, herons flying overhead, a lone farmer walking along a dike. What makes it more than an illustration is a wash of late afternoon light, mellow and elegiac. I am hooked. The gallery director, Ni Wayan Suarniti, knows it. My effort to bargain down the $400 asking price is doomed. I'm a poor man, I say. All Americans are rich, she answers; besides, we have expenses in our gallery. "Yes," I say, "but what about my expenses? I flew halfway around the world to get here!" It's no use. I have already left one painting behind in Bali. I won't repeat that mistake. The artist, Gusti Agung Galuh, arrives by motorbike to say hello and sign the back of the painting. Daughter of one painter, wife of another, she tells me she loves the same time of day that I do, when the last light slants into a well-ordered world, harmonious, balanced, quietly celebrated in her work. I will take her painting back home, where I hope it will accomplish what Bali itself still does: washing my eyes.

Dawn in Hawaii

National Geographic Traveler October/November 2016

If you dream of islands, dream of how they are at dawn, on the border between night and day, sleep and waking. Dream of them when they are cool and hushed, before heat and light chase the dream away. I learned this lesson — you could say it dawned on me — years ago. It's been confirmed many times since, across the Pacific and around the world.

It's still dark in Honolulu as I head on a highway that takes me to the eastern side of Oahu, past black basalt boulders and blowholes, waves geysering into the air. I stop at Sandy Beach, where locals greet the new day, some of them blowing conch shells to welcome morning. I continue to Waimanalo, where I find a beach, shaded by casuarina trees, that goes on for miles. Then I drive uphill on the Pali Highway and turn onto Old Pali Road, which runs through a rain forest, a tunnel with eucalyptus trees meeting overhead, mosses, vines, blossoms. It is cool and green and quiet. A perfect morning in paradise.

"Where America's Day Begins" is a slogan associated with Guam. It also applies to nearby Saipan, eight hours west of Hawaii by plane, across the international date line. Now part of the U.S. Commonwealth of the Northern Marianas, Saipan was a World War II battleground, and traces of that war — pillboxes, rusted landing craft — are everywhere. I first went to this island as a Peace Corps volunteer. I had requested Ethiopia or Turkey. I was sent to Saipan. It changed my life. I fell in love with the place. I've returned many times, to see how the lives of people I know are turning out and whether the battered, beautiful island still casts its spell. When I'm back, I'm up at dawn, driving along a coast lined with red-blossoming flame trees. I turn onto a bumpy road that brings me to Wing Beach just when the rising sun shines on the foaming crests of waves crashing in from the Philippine Sea. It's a new day's baptism.

South of Saipan, in Palau, dawn is indispensable, a time of awakening, with dogs and roosters sounding off, old women heading to taro patches, men tinkering with nets, spears, and outboard motors. It's a birth and blessing that lasts until the heat of morning rolls in as implacably and almost as wetly as the tide. Yet dawn here is not about temperature. It's about the smothering thickness of the air. You might be wearing a T-shirt, shorts, and flip-flops, but you feel like you're swathed in winter clothing. The occasional breezes are Mother Nature's insincere condolences. Warning: If you see people using umbrellas to shield themselves from sunlight, not rain, you're in trouble.

Dawn is when you plan your day, your future; sunset is when you contemplate your past. Too often dawn is missed, even in places where daybreak is the very heart, not just the start, of each day. Fly into the center of Australia, and you find dawn at its most winning. Here, in a vast emptiness, sits Uluru, a big hunk of red sandstone that rises more than a thousand feet and descends as many feet, or more, below ground, in an arid plain. Its size and solitude, and its place in local creation stories, make it sacred to Australia's Aboriginal people and entrancing to me.

In a hotel near Uluru I awaken well before sunrise and am dazzled by a sky that has more stars by far than I've ever seen. Put them in dry, clear air, no trace of pollution or urban glow, and here the stars ambush you. Uluru is out there in the darkness somewhere. I drive toward it, park, and approach the sandstone monolith on foot. Ever so slowly the sky becomes a little less black, then turns gray. The colossus declares itself. It feels like a living thing. It pulses colors: purple, then stark red, then orange, yellow, brown. I move closer to the magic, start running around the rock. Energized, I jog past small caves and sacred springs. I have Uluru to myself.

Then daylight arrives. Cars and vans begin to fill the parking lot. Some carry tourists determined to climb to the top of Uluru, a vulgar, sometimes fatal display of egotism that is officially discouraged but not quite prohibited. With heat come the flies, all around me, slow hungry things, a half dozen exploring the netting that hangs from my cap and shields my face.

Photographers have told me that sunrises and sunsets are interchangeable. Look-alikes. Most people love sunsets. They position themselves on patios and porches, at beaches and taverns, for happy hour, with fireworks across the horizon, captivating until the call for dinner. But to me it's no contest. Dawn is when the world is at its best, a fine and private place. Breakfast, and everything after, can wait.

On Island Time

Islands Magazine, August 1997

"Time," wrote Henry David Thoreau, "is but the stream I go a-fishing in." A lovely image — and misleading. It pictures time as quick and playful, a force of nature that can nonetheless be tamed, dammed, diverted.

Some years ago in the outer islands of the Yap district of Micronesia, on an atoll you could walk around in half an hour, I came across a grave marker, a flat concrete slab just off a trail. It didn't look like a local grave. For one thing, the name on it — Paul Glaser — was foreign, though the islands were full of foreign names, from Bismarck to Elvis. But island graves were in churchyards or, more commonly, next to houses, in plots edged by Coke and beer bottles stuck in the sand, garlanded with flower leis, both real and plastic.

That was something I liked, that custom of burying on the property, the idea of generations linking up in one place, as if the dead were still on call for babysitting. There was no thought of moving out and on. Instead what I noticed was a confidence that time wouldn't change things, a faith that people stayed put.

Yet this tradition made the lonely grave I'd found more puzzling. What was it doing there, all by itself, just above the water's edge, like something the tide had brought in.

Eventually, someone came along to tell me the grave belonged to a sailor who'd come in on a German cruiser, the Kormoran, during World War I. The ship had anchored right off-shore, he said. Then came the part that struck me, a gesture from someone not much older than I was, and no more likely than I to remember the Kormoran. "It stretched from here," he said, "to there." He pointed to a palm tree, well down the beach. It was as if he'd seen the Kormoran himself, as if nothing had happened since to cloud that memory, as if half a century were nothing.

And he was right. On islands, time isn't a passing stream, it's a surrounding ocean. News is what happens elsewhere, and history is what comes in off the sea, as a war or a typhoon, every 50 years or so. And sails away.

Island time is different time: deep, vast, oceanic. It's not controlled; it's not contained. It contains us. At home we measure time. We subdivide it like so much property. We sell it by the year or quarter-hour. On islands, time measures us and, frequently, finds us wanting. This is how it has been and still · is, though times — and time — are changing. The world makes inroads: Airports are beachheads of contemporaneity, tightly scheduled. Hotels are rented for so many days and nights. Tours run along as planned. On the day you arrive, your departure is ordained: It's like having a birth certificate with the date of death filled in.

You're a short-timer. You're closed-ended, and you sense it from the start: Just off the plane, watching returning islanders wrestle stenciled cardboard boxes off conveyor belts, you reach out for something small and stylish, leather and canvas, and perhaps some golf clubs or scuba gear. Just passing through, your baggage screams. Be back at the airport before you know it. If, for islanders, land is limited and time is infinite, for travelers, the world is wide and time is precious. The clock's always ticking; it's a sign of life, a vital sign, the next thing to a heartbeat. If you're lucky, island time will get to you. You'll begin to feel a difference between here and there, a certain delicious vagueness. It's hard to say what it is precisely. You almost don't want to analyze it, fearing it might go away. It's not the fact that you're visiting while lots of people are working. It's not just that magazines and newspapers and movies come in from elsewhere and take their time about it. It's not just distance and perspective. Those things count, but there is something deeper. It's the difference between a calendar and a tide table, between the march of time and the swing of a pendulum.

Island time isn't for everyone. Some travelers quickly yearn for familiar rhythms, deadlines, schedules. Before long, it's time for them to end their vacation, to go home primed to report on the time of their life. But there's a chance that you'll get hooked on island time, that you'll be drawn into a kind of rapture of the deep. Your short-timer identity confines you, you'll feel. Nationality, race, and class become exasperating barriers you want to cross.

It's out there, somewhere, an island inner life — secretive, oral, closely held, beyond your reach. It's a club you wonder about joining. You wonder about staying. You suspect you can't. Two kinds of life divide you, two kinds of time. They seem irreconcilable. And yet there is this: You can always return.

Forget island-hopping or island-collecting. Return to one place. Return after the tourist attractions are exhausted, after all the shopping's been done and the food isn't such a treat anymore. Return. Convert from one kind of time to another. Show up, time and time again. Don't travel by the clock; travel like the tide. Note the puzzlement and wonder that accompany your second and third appearances, the comparisons you start making, the discoveries that befall you, the beginnings of a life-enriching tension between two kinds of time. Be thankful, then, that there's room enough on earth for both of them. After that, begin to worry. It might not always be so.

There's a tension between island time and the time the rest of the world keeps. If the issue were joined, there's no kidding ourselves about which would win. And, if it comes to that, if the islands get scheduled, phased, and cellular, any number of islanders would applaud the change. To many of them — the younger, the educated, the movers and shakers — time is money.

What visitors come to cherish, some islanders hasten to abandon. You're coming in, they point out, and what you've just learned to value, they've learned to leave.

Nobody's fault, this crossing of paths and purposes, this difference in perspectives. Remember that high school game: conjugating adjectives? I'm robust, you're chunky, he's fat. Consider the language in island travel brochures.

Consider how the very qualities that are advertised to visitors might look to islanders — how "remote" translates to out-of-the-way, "unspoiled" to stillborn, "sleepy" to comatose, "quaint" to clueless. And "timeless"! It can mean eternal, constant, archetypal, or transient, negligible, off the clock. It can feel like a touch of eternity or a life sentence. I end with a confession. Ever since my first contact with islands — I was in my twenties then — I've divided the time in my life into two categories. There is time in the islands, the ones I keep returning to: Palau, Pohnpei, Saipan. And time away. That's the whole rest of my life. When I am away, I wonder what's going on back there. Not much, I hope. Then again, I'm an outsider. I suspect that no news is good news — and none of the news I've gotten has proved me wrong. Still, good or bad, these reports from small far places fascinate me.

And if we grant that measuring a day in the life of an island is sampling the ocean with an eyedropper, we have William Blake to remind us "to see a world in a grain of sand... and eternity in an hour." An island poet, no doubt about it.

Pacific Retreats — America's Best Kept Secret

National Geographic Traveler, September 2007, Volume 24, No. 6

Somewhere west of Hawaii, a tourist becomes a traveler. Granted, Hawaii is fine. I need that feeling of relaxation as soon as I step off the plane in Honolulu — to take a deep breath of island air, knowing that several time zones now separate me from all the things I worry about.

For most people, Hawaii is as far as they come. For me it's a halfway point. West of Hawaii, in a huge swath of the Pacific, there are more than 2,000 islands bound in one way or another to the United States. From the east, they stretch from southernmost American Samoa to the northerly Marshalls and Marianas to Palau in the far west.

I first came to this part of the world as a Peace Corps volunteer in the late 1960s. "The Peace Corps Goes To Paradise," the recruiting advertisement read. I was assigned to Saipan, in the Northern Marianas, where I attended picnics, weddings, cockfights. I edited a government magazine from an office on Capitol Hill, which the Trust Territory government had inherited from the C.I.A. I picnicked on the World War II invasion beach, boon-docked into war-littered caves on the north end of the island, stayed up late in bars where you could still hear "You Are My Sunshine." That's when I developed a lifelong need for small, obscure places, a passion that's a lot like gambling. In Hawaii, you know what you're getting. In the islands beyond, you never know. It's travel, island travel, serendipitous and untogether. You take your chances: Will there be someone to meet you at the airport? Will the rental car have a spare tire? Perhaps not. Will anyone know you are coming? Maybe, maybe not.

In the islands, all life processes are ratcheted up a notch. My hair grows more quickly. I need to shave more often, and I swear, my fingernails need more frequent clipping. I'm in closer touch with my body, welcoming that half hour of cool, just around sunrise, and toughing out the middle of the day and waiting for that wonderful time in the late afternoon when a breeze kicks up, shadows lengthen, sunlight mellows, and the place is golden.

Some of the best meals I've ever had were in the islands. There's a hotel on Pohnpei that does a mangrove crab that I can't imagine finding anywhere else, and a steak coated with fresh local pepper, and a soursop ice cream. On Saipan, I seek out a local specialty, kelaguin, which combines grated coconut, shredded chicken, hot peppers, green onions, and lemon juice, a cool but spicy meal, nicely accompanied by saffron rice. In Palau, with luck, I can find demok, a soup involving taro leaves, coconut milk, and crab or chicken. But let's talk about fish, glorious fish. People here are fussy about fish the way the French are fussy about wine and cheese. Fresh fish out of a pristine sea: It doesn't get any better. Picture slivers of sashimi off a fish that was caught five minutes before, dipped in a sauce of soya , lemon, wasabi mustard. The best fish I remember was in Palau, late in the afternoon, when some politicians I worked for lit a fire under a piece of discarded corrugated metal, threw a fish on top, and we ate it with our fingers. Those are things you miss about the islands when you're away.

From the Honolulu airport, my flight heads west, out over the largest of oceans, aiming for the smallest of islands, headed to a kind of home. It begins at check-in, where I see dark- or tan-skinned islanders wrestling luggage to the counter, not golf bags, surfboards, or matching suitcases, but taped-up cardboard boxes with island addresses Magic-Markered on the outside: the Republic of the Marshall Islands; Kosrae , Pohnpei, Chuuk, and Yap in the Federated States of Micronesia; the Republic of Palau; the Commonwealth of the Northern Mariana Islands.

I glimpse loose, loudly flowered dresses, and I hear languages that I can recognize, though not speak. I catch a whiff of pomade, maybe coconut oil. And then there are the faces, often resembling people I know or used to know. Some are dead, others are older now, but the eyes and mouths and voices of old friends keep showing up, in their relatives and descendants. I notice wads of betelnut neatly buried in sand-filled ashtrays in the smoking area outside. It feels familiar. I'm not sure whether I chose the place or it chose me. Or whether it's something that just happened. An accident. But something keeps me coming back, beyond Hawaii.

I visit new islands, and increasingly go back to old ones, to see how things — lives, landscapes — are turning out. That's what is special about this Pacific region. It's exotic, remote, obscure. It is also, over time, domestic, so that on each return, I feel like I'm catching up on a story — part mystery, part comedy, large part soap opera — that I've missed a few episodes of. Bali Ha'i meets Peyton Place: a potent combination. Give it time and it takes over, like an addiction. It gets to the point where you divide your life into two parts — 1. the years you spend among the islands, and 2. other stuff.

The United States doesn't exactly run or own all of these islands — an incoming American would find it almost impossible to buy land here (although you can visit easily without a visa) — but they are as close as America will come to a Pacific domain: half a million people on a total land mass smaller than Rhode Island. Acquired at the turn of the 20th century, Guam and American Samoa are US territories. Micronesia came to us after World War II, was administered as a UN trust territory, and eventually splintered into the Commonwealth of the Northern Marianas, the Federated States of Micronesia, the Republics of Palau and the Marshall Islands. All the islands concede military rights to the US and count on it for money and government programs. All islanders can freely travel to the US and enlist in the US military. They're discovering the US more all the time. But, except for a few aging veterans and former government workers, some ex-Peace Corps volunteers, a handful of anthropologists and divers, America doesn't know these islands.

They are, to be sure, tiny places. Check out the Marshall Islands from above, look down on Majuro or Kwajalein, and you'll see how small: fragile filaments of sand and palm tenuously attached to coral reefs. But then, in Kosrae and Pohnpei, in the eastern Carolines, you encounter something entirely different: cloud-covered rain-forested mountains, hulking and muscular. Not many sand beaches are here: Thickets of mangroves ring the islands. Chuuk — formerly Truk — mixes low islands and high, all in a vast lagoon, with a sunken Japanese fleet reposing on the bottom. In the Marianas there are the battle-scarred islands of Saipan and Tinian. Down south, in the western Carolines, Yap — quietest of all the islands — offers the closest encounter a visitor can have with the way things used to be. And then there's Palau — the epicenter of my obsession — a turbulent, sassy, scheming place. All my island musings end in Palau.

Whenever I return to Palau, I have to make sure the magic is still there. Before dawn, groggy from the long westward flight across datelines and time zones, I drive through the streets of Koror, the main city, and head out toward Malakai Harbor, past warehouses, bars, barracks, gas stations, convenience stores that warn me never to use the word paradise to describe Pacific islands. And, all of a sudden, the road dips, ends, and makes a liar out of me: Paradise confronts me as I face the northern edge of a flotilla of densely-wooded coral islands — the so-called "Rock Islands" — that stretch for miles, all the way down to the World War II battleground of Peleliu. This is a realm of winding channels, unscalable cliffs, hidden beaches, secret passages. As the sky turns gray, the islands separate themselves from sea and stars and the morning sun offers shades of blue and green that I would — that I have — traveled halfway around the world to see again. In these islands, there's a blend of land and sea, a play of darkness and light, that remains in the mind forever. I know how my Palauan friends weary of outsiders telling them that they live in paradise, their islands are beautiful, they should not change a thing. Things are bound to change. But please, I say, not this.

Conversation with Palauans takes practice. And endurance. Nothing is brisk, businesslike, linear and logical. Gossip, history, speculation, scandal commingle: Sticking to an agenda is like walking into a yard sale with a shopping list. From morning to midnight, over coffee, over mangrove crabs, fish and taro, gallons of beer and yards of sashimi, I immerse my self in the talk of the town. And the talk is all about the Republic's new national capitol. People want me to see it. They want to know what I think of it — I can tell I'm being tested. And I suspect they're not sure what they think of it themselves.

I drive across a bridge donated by the Japanese, turn onto a 53-mile highway financed by the U.S., and head toward the new capitol, largely funded by Taiwan. I'm on Babeldaob, Palau's largest island, green and empty, with terraced hillsides, dense forests, mangrove thickets, taro patches, and tapioca plantings. Before the bridge, going to Babeldaob took a boat driver, good weather, a tube of sunblock, a stout heart, and a long day. Now, I coast through sleepy villages, along a breezy palm-fringed shoreline, open beaches. "Millionaires come from far away to sleep under a palm tree," a young man goofing off once told me. "Why not me?" I've lost count of my returns to Palau, I reflect. A dozen or more, for sure. Why so many, when there are so many other places left to see? It's something about Palauans, I suppose, their conviction that those small islands are special, the center of the world, and that they are special people. They believe it, and they made a believer out of me.

And then I see what the Palauans want me to see: Washington, D.C., transplanted. Executive, legislative, and judicial offices, not mock-ups or scale models, but full-sized, three stories high, with marble floors and air-conditioning. And it's true: I don't know what to think. The capitol might be considered a tribute to democracy and the proof of alliance with America. Or, as one commentator puts it, "the most architecturally inappropriate… building in the world." What will I say to the Palauans? And then, as I'm staring at a gleaming white dome, it comes to me, the wisest saying ever about these islands: "The Spanish came for God, the Germans for gold, the Japanese came for glory. And the Americans came for good."

"This is the way Hawaii used to be." That's what people say about the Federated States of Micronesia (Yap, Chuuk, Pohnpei, Kosrae). But it isn't clear how long it's been since Hawaii looked like, say, Yap, where men walk through shady villages on ancient stone paths, wearing loincloths and chewing betel nut. 1875? Or maybe 1941: Consider the Japanese fleet sunk in the Chuuk Lagoon. And what era comes to mind on gorgeous Pohnpei, where you find dogs on offer at island luaus? Or when, on Kosrae, thanks to long-ago missionaries, you not only can't buy a beer on Sunday, you also can't be caught consuming one?

This is where travel requires a change in perspective, a shift of gears. "Every time I go back," says Karen Peacock, a University of Hawaii curator, "halfway through the trip, I have to tell myself, 'Slow down, you're talking too fast, you're moving too fast.' In the islands there's a slowness in movement, a slowness in the cadence of voices. You can't rush people or things. You can't make things happen."

In Yap, a visitor proceeds carefully through villages. Don't even think of swimming on a beach or taking a picture of a topless woman without permission, which might be refused. This is not a place that panders. You learn to ask, to step quietly. And you work the edges of the day — those cool mornings and late afternoons, those heavy, velvety evenings. The middle of the day is a write-off.

In Chuuk, you snorkel and dive the sunken fleet and at night, stay close to your hotel. There's little else to do. And in Kosrae, there's also nothing to do. Here, it's meant as a compliment. "It's the greenest island I've ever seen," says one visitor. "They've got tons of local food... tangerines, bananas, oranges... pleasant walks, congenial conversations." Another person tells me this about Kosrae: "There are centuries-old ruins, there's Mount Finkol to climb, there's snorkeling and diving. And there's the smell you get after it rains, the sense that everything is growing right around you. Only you can't get a beer on Sunday."

You can't get a beer but you can go to church, on Kosrae, Pohnpei, Chuuk, Yap, or in the Marshalls, and you'll never forget it. Sit inside or stand around outside and listen to the congregation sing. It's harmonic, high-pitched, plaintive, keening, nasal.

It's an anthem for all the world's small places, and if you hear it once, you hear it forever.

Pohnpei, location of the capital of the Federated States, is a green, hulking island, with ridge after ridge of rain-forested mountains. Attend to its sounds. The crow of roosters, the barking of dogs in mornings. The wind, when you climb up an old Japanese road past rusted gun emplacements that the rain forest has turned into tropical planters, out to the front of Sokehs Rock, Pohnpei's Diamond Head. There's the blitz of mosquitos zapping onto the electric coil behind the bar of the Village Hotel: Who needs television? There's the rhythmic beat that comes out of Pohnpei bars sakau bars, where the root of a pepper shrub is pounded on rocks, strained through hibiscus bark, and ritually served to a waiting circle of drinkers. It's Pohnpei's traditional drink — some would say its communal narcotic — a spicy, earthy concoction that numbs and mellows. There's the sound — the sound of silence — you get when you voyage to Pohnpei's prehistoric Venice — the ruins of Nan Madol, a 92-island complex of tombs, temples, and canals, eerie and somber on the brightest of days, impossible to think of visiting at night. There's the sound of waterfalls. And then there's the sound of rain on this180-inches-a-year island. It's like nowhere else. It accelerates from first drops to flood in seconds, rolls off of thatch roofs, drums on metal. Coconuts come down like cannonballs, and just when you think it's raining as hard as it can, it finds a final surge. It goes on for hours, diminuendo and crescendo. But it's always sunny — and steamy — in the morning.

Most planes that fly across Micronesia stop at Majuro, capital of the Republic of the Marshall Islands. Depending on whether you're headed east or west, Majuro is your first or last sight of the islands. Prologue or epilogue. And what matters most is what you see from the air as you head in to Majuro, an atoll 25 miles long and, in places, no wider than the length of a football field. '"You wonder how people could live there," says one visitor. "And everywhere you drive, you look one way, you've got the lagoon; the other way, the ocean. You cross a bridge, maybe ten or so feet above the water, and they tell you it's the highest point on the island." And there's something else that you notice, a sense of nowhere-to-go, nothing-to-do that you detect on any small island. But it seems stronger here.

That image of smallness, true of all these islands, is even more true of Majuro, smallness and vulnerability, of being at the mercy of whoever comes across the sea — missionaries, businessmen, Japanese soldiers, American Marines, and, just recently, Chinese, who by some counts operate most of the island's stores. Though most travelers are unlikely to linger in Majuro, some visitors love the buzz and gossip of the place, the Doonesbury cast of politicians and schemers who crowd the bars at night. But my favorite moment comes in the late afternoon, when the Marshallese stroll along the roads, sit outside stores, walking and talking slowly, like passengers on a ship that is way out at sea.

Majuro is unlikely to attract travelers who aren't headed — quickly — to outlying atolls, like Arno, ten miles away: no electricity, no television, no hot water, few if any cars. Or, better yet, Bikini, a diver's mecca. An aircraft carrier, the USS Saratoga, and a Japanese flagship, the Nagato, sit waiting on the floor of the lagoon, sunk in nuclear tests. If Bikini's not in your plans, watch carefully as your flight approaches Kwajelein, a missile test site. Ask the flight attendant to ask the pilot to tell you when you're above another famous battleship, Germany's Prinz Eugen, which rests in the shallows, its propellers well above the water.

American Samoa "is probably the most isolated place in America," says David Cohen, a Department of the Interior official who is half Samoan. "It's American Polynesia!" It's hard to accept that a place called Pago Pago is a permanent part of the United States. American Samoa draws far fewer visitors than its larger neighbor, independent Samoa, where you can visit Robert Louis Stevenson's home, Villa Vailima, and climb up to his grave, with its famous epitaph ("Home is the sailor, home from the sea, And the hunter home from the hill").

In American Samoa, you can venerate a prostitute named Sadie Thompson, immortalized in Somerset Maugham's short story, "Rain," and embodied in films by Rita Hayworth and Joan Crawford. The Sadie Thompson Inn — a hotel and bar restaurant — is said to occupy the site of Sadie's business. And from there you can journey to outlying villages and to the new National Park of American Samoa, with tropical forests, coral reefs, flying foxes. You can also learn a lesson or two about islands. Samoans have been dealing with the United States for over a century — pretty shrewdly — and the relationship has a steadiness that's missing in other places. "They're proud of being Samoans, and they're proud of being Americans," says Cohen, "and they somehow make it work!" Samoans are committed to fa'asamoa, the Samoan way, an attachment to tradition, family, respect, and reciprocity. It's hard to define.

"I once judged a California Miss Samoa contest," says Cohen, "and we asked all of the contestants to define fa'asamoa. One contestant responded, 'Every other Friday, I get my paycheck and give it all to my mother. That's fa'asamoa!" Attached as they may be to the Samoan way, island rootedness is matched by island restlessness. There are 60,000 American Samoans at home... and 90,000 Samoans in the United States. Right now, a young American Samoan is 18 times as likely as a mainland youth to die in a U.S. military uniform in Iraq, and 34 times as likely to play in the National Football League. Paradise: Love it or leave it. Those 90,000 Samoans in the US are scrambling for jobs — and lives that their home islands can't provide. Remember me, their home islands seem to say, to the people who left them and the ones who come to visit.

It's possible to fly into and out of the places I've mentioned and, if all the connections click, you could do it in a couple of weeks or so. And miss almost everything worth seeing. The region takes time, tests patience. The main islands are only the beginning; they are the only place to begin, but they are not the end. There are thousands of islands out there, divided into the easy to get to, the difficult, the damned near impossible. The easy ones are connected by major airlines to Honolulu, Guam, Manila, Tokyo. The difficult can be reached by local airlines, and, in some cases, small boats. But the vast majority are the damn near impossible. Those are the ones that break your heart, especially if you saw them once and swore that you'd go back. Every time you glance at a map, they reproach you. They dance into range: You hear about a boat, a private plane. Then, as schedules change, money runs out, weather intervenes, they skip away again.

South of Pohnpei, there are a couple of magic-sounding atolls that call to me — Kapingamarangi and Nukuoro. North of Saipan, there's a recently-active volcano called Pagan. Outside Chuuk, in the Mort locks, is Satawan, where I'm told, the men stand on the reef on moonlit nights, holding umbrellas, and harvest lobsters that come seeking shade. South of Palau, there's a lonely raft of scrub and sea at a place called Helen Reef, a bird and turtle haven; a wrecked fishing boat, the Nagasaki Naru, sits on the vast reef. There's rocky, lonely Fais, in the state of Yap, where I saw kids in red loincloths skipping over rusted mining equipment. It was like a movie about people surviving the end of the world.

These are remote islands, hard catches. When you've been to them — and I've been to two of the above — you never forget them. And if you've tried and failed, they obsess you. It's a schedule-wrenching, budget-rupturing diversion, but if you hear of a boat or a plane, public or private, headed outside the reef, consider taking it. Granted, it may prolong your trip. It could last a lifetime.

I've given my island obsession years and how many islands have I visited? Fewer than one hundred, I'm sure: 60 sounds about right. I doubt that anyone in the state where I live, or in any neighboring states, can match that total. I might be the champion visitor to our distant Pacific cousins. So what? Who's counting? I am. Who cares? I do. So I keep going back.

Pacific Islands

National Geographic Traveler, October 1999

This love of islands gets embarrassing. I just phoned my travel agent and, while on hold waiting to learn whether I could get from Columbus, Ohio to the Pacific islands of Palau for less than $3,000, I listened to a taped message that recounted tropical island charms: swaying palms, balmy breezes, white-sand beaches, underwater wonderlands, Technicolor sunsets. It made me wince. Can anyone say the word "paradise" without a wised-up grin? We all know better, don't we? And yet, with whole continents still unvisited, I keep returning to a small, remote place I've seen a dozen times before.

Why? I was 25 when I fell in love with Palau. I was a Peace Corps volunteer in Micronesia, assigned to Saipan, north of Guam. I liked Saipan fine. But I kept hearing about Palau. With my first sight of that island archipelago — hulking, mangrove-fringed Babelthuap; the rooftops and causeways of the old Japanese colonial capital of Koror; the flotilla of tiny limestone islets stretching down toward the World War II battlegrounds of Peleliu and Angaur — my life was changed forever. Palau was poaching, plant-smelling air; liquid, velvety nights; shades of blue and green I'd never seen before. It was a daily awareness of light and heat, land and sea, sweat and rain, growth and decay. It was people, a community that was part Bali Hai, part Peyton Place — gossipy, conspiratorial, and not pleased at hearing from outsiders that they were living in Paradise.

Most islands have an offshore feel. They're a short flight or a ferry ride from larger places. But, like other Pacific islands, Palau is out there, the end of the line, a dot of land in the world's largest sea. Its greatest gift is the delicious sense that you've gotten as far away as is possible from the rest of your life. In Palau, I walk around giddy, thinking of the people back home. "If they could see me now," I'm pleased to tell myself, knowing that they can't. With time, I've developed some theories about small islands. Not theories. Laws. Everything is connected. Things die down, not out; nothing is ever over. And one more: The more you leave behind — work, career, possessions, all your mainland occupations — the better is your taste of islands. Sure, I concede there's something cliched about this love of islands, something that smacks of shipwreck cartoons and purple prose. There's also something youthful about the writers who have been this way before — Melville, Stevenson, Michener — that may make them easy to discount. Still, once again I pass on other places and point toward Palau, as though rereading a book I've read before, sighing over what I marked and underlined when I was younger, worrying about it when I am there, wondering about it when I'm gone.

Palau: The Age of Barbecue

Pilgrims & Natives, Idaho State University Journal of Arts & Letters, Spring 2004, Vol. 38, No. 2

KLUGE VISITS AGAIN. Front page, below the fold, there I am. My umpteenth farewell visit to the islands of Palau is a story, at least in the islands of Palau. The weekly *Tia Belau* informs its readers that a former Micronesia Peace Corps volunteer, friend of a late former president, author of two books set in Palau, has returned once again to visit these Pacific islands and meet with old friends. The story is fine, as far as it goes. Measured by the standards of high school journalism — the four W's — it has the who, the what, the where of the story. But not the why.

Why, when I am half a world away and half a lifetime older than when I first arrived, do I find myself wondering about Palau, about how lives are turning out across the Pacific, how elections are being fought, deals are being made? About all the alarms and skirmishes of a place that no one I know — students, fellow professors — has heard about, unless from me? Why is it that I miss the pre-dawn tropical cool or the heavy velvet feel of the air at night? What was it about the last leg of this journey, that southward flight from Guam to Palau, that turned me so thoughtful, this odd mix of joy and mourning? Was it the vastness of the sea below? The depths, in this part of the Pacific, that could drown an Everest? The smallness of my landing place, tiny islands exotic as Bali Hai, entangled as Peyton Place? And what about the homecoming glee I felt when I saw fellow passengers, people I knew or sort of knew, reaching for air sickness bags, leaning forward to spit out blood-colored gobs of betelnut juice? It's as though I was entering into a magnetic zone, a field of force. I can't count the times that, in flying to other places, I've found myself wishing that I was headed here. KLUGE VISITS AGAIN, filled with wonder and chagrin, all sorts of might-have-beens about Palauans and Palau and me.

In 1969, actor Lee Marvin appeared on the Tonight Show to publicize "Hell in the Pacific," a World War II story filmed in Palau. I'd freelanced a location piece for Life magazine that Johnny Carson had asked about.'"A wet-behind-the-ears Ph.D.," Marvin called me. Sharp eyed, sneaky-smart, Marvin had me down. I'd asked the Peace Corps to send me to Ethiopia or Turkey — I'd been reading Lawrence Durrell. They sent me to Micronesia, then known as the Trust Territory of Pacific Islands, a slew of small places the United States had captured from the Japanese and was administering, sort of, as a United Nations Trusteeship.

There was. no Lawrence Durrell for Micronesia, just some magazine articles and a short litany of facts I soon memorized: 2,141 islands aggregating half the size of Rhode Island scattered over an area the size of the continental United States; 120,000 inhabitants — you could seat all of them in the Rose Bowl — with nine mutually-unintelligible languages, a history of colonization that went from Spain to Germany to Japan to the USA. The Americans had passed the baton from the Navy to the Department of Interior which was now joined by Kennedy's children, the can-do gung-ho Peace Corps.

I had gotten about as far away from the United States as it was possible to get and yet, exotic as the islands were, they were also American, secured by Marines who'd left "blood on the reef" and remained, some of them, in the Trust Territory government. The government budget came from Washington, its current leader —"the high commissioner" was from Hawaii. Not that we were colonists. Perish the thought, that wasn't our mission at all. Our agreement with the United Nations specified that Micronesia would be led to "self-government or independence," somehow, sometime. Meanwhile, America was on the ground, in the air. Hordes of big-eyed kids were learning English in tin-roofed classrooms, while older brothers returned home from universities in Guam and Hawaii with political science degrees. Cars and movies, canned fish and fried chicken, outboard motors, fiberglass boats, cement-block homes and air-conditioned offices, American infrastructure, fads and fashions claimed the place, winning hearts and minds. Quo vadis, Micronesia? Quo vadis, Palau? There were going to be some testing negotiations between Micronesia and America, that was clear. As the world measured stories, these islands didn't amount to much. "There are only 120,000 people out there," Henry Kissinger was quoted as saying. "Who gives a damn?"

I gave a damn. When I look back, I'm inclined to concede that I might have fallen in love with wherever I was sent. But it felt different in 1967. It was as if the islands were waiting for me. The day I arrived, maybe the day before, they owned me forever. Everywhere, landscape and characters came together, visions and voices, but nowhere more powerfully than Palau. It was as if I'd stepped into something — a Jacobean drama, a situation comedy or maybe one of those experimental dramas that break down the barrier between actor and audience, stage and seat. The Palauans have a welcoming dance — I saw it for the first time when I was escorting Lee Marvin — a half chant, half song accompanied by a clapping of hands, followed by first one woman, then another approaching guests, extending a hand, leading them on to the floor and into a swaying, pounding bump and grind. It was impossible to decline the invitation, impossible to perform without feeling foolish. That, I learned, was how the place worked. What comes next is my account of my particular foolishness, which was also my particular dream.

I learned there were two ways for an outsider to engage with Palau. Neither was foolproof. There were outsiders, mostly Americans, who became Palauan, or at least they tried. They married local women, lived in the villages, spoke a little of the language, fished and drank beer with their in-laws and friends. Empty Budweisers rolled around their rusted pick-up trucks, their teeth and shirts were stained with betelnut, and they kept low profiles, speaking about fishing, not politics. Their tenure in paradise was happy but, after adjusting for climate, landscape, food and lots of other important things, they might have been living in Oklahoma.

My dream was different and it's easy to say, riskier. The point was not to become a Palauan. For one thing, you'd never pass. Sure, you could get by forever, if you watched your step. The moment you asserted yourself, though, you'd get this look: "Who is this man? Where is he from? What village? Who was his mother?" You'd be another long-nosed foreigner, tolerated at best. What's more, there was no shortage of Palauans in Palau. Imitation was flattering, not interesting. No, I saw myself as living as an American in Palau, and an American writer going far, going deep for stories that would reach readers everywhere. Palau would be my Paris and my Yoknapatawpha County, my literary turf. I pictured a house on a hill overlooking the islands, the lagoon, the barrier reef. There'd be one air-conditioned room at the center of my home, mostly for the sake of cameras, stereos, books and papers, though the prospect of an afternoon nap that didn't leave me lying in a puddle of sweat couldn't be discounted. The rest of the house was all porch, with a cook shed and lean-to shower in the back. There'd be a metal roof that would creak at sunrise, contract at dusk, that the rain would drum on while I typed below. Palau had endless stories, I was sure. Islands were small places and, to the rest of the world, small meant simple: nice to visit and easy to know. The world was wrong. Palau was an imploded universe of complication, with unwritten history, invisible borders, buried feuds, alliances, betrayals and ambitions. Unlike most small towns, Palau was surrounded by the sea; had seen wars, lived with and learned from four foreign administrations. Palau drew dreamers, hustlers, carpetbaggers, some from Asia and the Pacific, many from the States: cranks, idealists, fugitives and con men, people who were vague about their past, businessmen and lawyers with clients, wives, and regulatory boards on their tails, characters who inspired a song that went something like this:

> Tell me, what was your name in the States?
> Was it Johnson or Jackson or Bates?
> Did you murder your wife? Did you run for your life?
> Tell me, what was your name in the States?

It wasn't just a dream of writing. It was about living in Palau. It was about friendships, back-channel and off-the-record, with the Palauans who'd run the place after the trusteeship ended, men like Lazarus Salii, Polycarp Basilius, Roman Tmetuchl, Kaleb Udui, John Ngiraked, lively, clever, curious men. I could picture knowing them, sharing their lives. Sharing life, as well, with a Palauan woman. It wasn't hard, picturing that, seeing myself with someone whose fascination with the world off island would mirror my own preoccupation with Palau. And with all of that, the house, the wife, the friends, I would nonetheless never kid myself that I was a Palauan. That was one mistake I'd never make. All I'd know was how they looked at me and I could make a career out of that.

It didn't happen. True, two Palau-based books came along and a half dozen magazine assignments and trips like this. Sometimes it feels stupid. Revisiting an old house, an old girlfriend once is poignant. Going back ten times feels retarded. That doesn't keep me away. It confirms what I concluded years ago was a rule of island life: nothing is ever over. Things die down. Not out.

At dawn, I drive through the streets of Koror. What was once all puddles and potholes is paved. There are stoplights now and policemen putting out traffic cones, regulating the flow of employees headed to work in what is Palau's largest industry: government. There are more buildings every time I return — a gas station on the site of the Royal Palauan Hotel, the leaky ribald quonset where Lee Marvin and I stayed. I miss the overhead fans chopping at smoke-filled air, the bar crowded with tropical characters, imported and local, geckos crawling on screens. How could I not have fallen in love with a ramshackle, tin-roofed town like Koror, where the Navy's quonsets mixed with shrines, offices, and docks the Japanese left behind? To the north lay Babeldaob, the big island, mangrove-lined, with ten major coastal villages and no roads. Just south of Koror was a flotilla of uninhabited limestone islands which, this first morning back, I urgently need to see again. I drive through the port area of Malakal, Chinese fishing boats at anchor, I pass barges and yachts, car-rental agencies, warehouses and foreign workers' barracks. It's still early: grouchy dogs are sleeping in the middle of the road, a bar girl walks home from someplace, plastic wrappers blow in front of my car. As I go down a last small hill, past Koror's sewage treatment plant, I come to a little water-slide park called Icebox. Behind me lies Koror, all the random hodgepodge of contemporary Palauan life, a confusing mix of energy and torpor I will spend a couple of weeks re-learning. Where I stand is a border between a place where the word paradise could not be used without a tiresome irony: paradise lost, paradise leased, trouble in paradise. In front of me, though, the old dream gets born every morning and paradise applies completely. What I see while sitting on a damp concrete picnic table is an artful blend of land and sea that makes the planet's big deals, oceans and broad continents seem coarse and simple-minded. Left, right and center are the Rock Islands, limestone hulks, sharply pitted and unclimbably steep, undercut along the waterline, festooned by trees and vines above. There are colors in these islands that I haven't seen anyplace else, greens and blues so intense that they make the rest of the world seem smudged and faded. I arrive just in time to see a night sky release its grip on the horizon, turn gray, while what's below stays black. I begin to make out the islands, three groups of them separated by channels leading from east and west into Malakai Harbor. It's a drawing in ink, charcoal, fog and smoke and then there's a purple bruise in the east — the future headed this way — followed by red and orange and the sun's first rays catching the uppermost ridges. After that it's like watching a photograph, the invention of technicolor, these greens and blues that reach full strength, and after that, just keep on coming. There are places in these islands that no one has ever gone to, there are narrow channels widening out into perfect coves, where your voice drops to the level of a whisper, you feel so much like an intruder. Just as the islands are set in a lagoon, circled by a barrier reef, so, too, in the middle of the rock islands themselves there are lakes, marine lakes connected by tenuous underground channels to the outside concentric circles of creation, from the smallest possible islands to the largest earthly sea.

A few days after I return, I head into the Rock Islands to the place where the modern history of Palau began. My companion is Arthur Ngiraklsong, an old friend who is the current Chief Justice of Palau. We met twenty-five years ago, when we were both staffers at the Micronesian Constitutional Convention, crafting a document for a union that Palau eventually declined to join. Ngiraklsong had been away, learning and practicing law in the United States. Our meeting coincided with the beginning of his return to Palau.

"You don't have to be smart to practice law," he often says. "You do have to be organized." He cuts a stern figure in court. He scares people. He keeps his distance from family and clan-based entanglements, local politics. It's likely Palauans find him unusual. He lives in a house many of his countrymen would shun: the first president of Palau, Haruo Remeliik, was assassinated at the edge of his driveway. He relishes the company of seven dogs who laze around his porch. What other Palauan would cook for their dogs, rice mixed with chicken or fish? I've always enjoyed his company. We exchange emails, betting on the Super Bowl, conjecturing whether Venus and Serena Williams might have some Palauan blood and, if so, from what specific village might they descend?

Now we meet at Koror's M dock, at the end of a causeway shared by a tourist hotel, a Japanese-built aquarium and the town garbage dump, which has caught fire these last few days, junk cars with gasoline left in them exploding as flames reach them. This is what we leave behind, heading into the Rock Islands, instantly feeling fine. If you're a visitor, you wonder if your enjoyment of the local landscape isn't tiresome — those greens! those blues! — to people who see it every day and hear it: the newcomer's heartfelt admonition not to change a thing, it's perfect just as it is. In Ngiraklsong, I have a companion who needs these places as much as I do and for the same reason.

No one lives in the Rock Islands, there are no hotels yet and it gives me pause that my first memory of Palau is of a place where no one lives, a disembodied landscape. Yet these islands are at the heart of things here. They're an escape from Koror. They are social places, private places. And, in an era of indiscriminate development, where money can accomplish anything, they are Palau's castle keep: one inviolable place. Without them, Palau is just another island on the make, a cargo cult looking skyward for tourist hotels, garment factories, military bases, you name it. But so long as these islands remain intact, it is possible to take seriously what Palauans believe, that they are special, God-gifted. Forget all sorts of evidence to the contrary, the course of history, the flow of information, the balance of trade, Palauans believe they are living at the center of the world. It's the first thing I noticed about them, their confidence and pride and the bemusement with which they regarded anyone who had the bad luck to be born someplace else. It wasn't always pleasing — it shaded into arrogance and attitude. In many individual cases — scowling, dead-eyed opportunists — it was hard to see what it was based on, what ability or experience. It was an article of faith, almost, you believed or you didn't. I believed.

We wind our way out of Malakai, rummaging among small islands, speeding through alleys between the islands, probing quiet coves and inlets, heading southwest, across the lagoon to the island of Ulong. We talk about Palau but soon we muse about other places: Norfolk Island, where I've been twice, draws Ngiraklsong. He wonders about the Pitcairn people, descendants of the Bounty mutineers, who live there. As for me, I'm dying to get into some infrequently visited islands southwest of Palau, especially an uninhabited bird and turtle island at a place called Helen Reef. I saw it once in 1976 and the heart-stopping loneliness of it — a few acres of sand and palm, inside a broad lagoon that had a Japanese fishing boat, the Nagasaki Maru, rusting on the reef — has stayed with me. If I return it had better be soon. A recent visitor showed me pictures indicating that the island is now a third the size of the already tiny place I saw. The coconut grove is gone; little more than a sandbar remains. And what magazine editor would send me to visit an uninhabited island about to slip away forever? I can see their eyes glaze over. That's the problem about islands. Making what matters to me matter to others. "The only way to live on an island is to travel," Ngiraklsong reflects. Though they are part of Palau, the Rock Islands are an escape from it as well. Again and again, I hear Palauans yearn for a respite from the closeness of island life. My friend is not immune. "I like to travel to a place where no one knows my name or who I am, where I come from, a place where I could die in the street and no one would care..."

Like the rest of the islands, Ulong is steep, thickly forested, its limestone foundations undercut at the waterline, with recessed shelves where crocodiles sometimes lurk. It has a long sandy beach on its southern side and there's a sheltered cove around the other side of the island. On August 9, 1873 both these features were crucial, when the East India packet ship Antelope, bound for Macao, crashed onto a Palauan reef. Captain Henry Wilson and his crew of fifty made their way onto Ulong's beach, salvaged what they could from the stranded vessel, which they eventually rebuilt in the island's cove. Two days after they landed, the Palauans came to them. There had been glancing encounters with Spaniards and Chinese going back two hundred years but this was Palau's first prolonged encounter with the outside world. And it went well. The Englishmen served tea and biscuits, displayed dogs and geese, introduced bronze and iron. The paramount Palauan chief, the Ibedul, offered shipbuilding manpower. The gift-giving escalated. Within a week of their arrival, English sailors and firearms accompanied the Ibedul in a fleet of 150 canoes, attacking a rival chief in north Babeldaob. This alliance led to the greatest gift of all: when the English departed after three months the Ibedul's son, Prince Lee Boo, went with them, back to London, where he charmed people with his quickness and grace. Smallpox killed him six months later but his name lived on in pageants and plays, on postage stamps, in a street name and — most important — in George Keate's best selling account of the Antelope. The monument at Lee Boo's grave bears a poet's inscription:

Stop, Reader, Stop!
Let Nature Claim a Tear —
A Prince of Mine, Lee Boo,
Lies Buried Here

Coleridge visited as well, wept and wrote:

My soul amid the pensive gloom
Mourn'd with the breeze, O Lee Boo,
o'er thy tomb

Arthur Ngiraklsong and I wade ashore on the shipwreck island, nod at picnicking Palauans and visiting skin divers. It's a fine beach, sandy and gentle at the edge, yielding to lush woods inland. We pass a historical marker and head inland to look, in vain, for a well left behind by the Antelope crew. The story of Wilson and Lee Boo casts a long shadow. The more I think about it, the more it forecasts Palau's relations with the world: the Palauan eagerness to deal, their way of turning foreign presence to local advantage, their restlessness and fascination with the world outside. Granted, later visitors were less well received. Warfare and disease decimated the place. Four foreign governments came and left without asking. But the experience of the Antelope still resonated. "A captain just doesn't take a stranger on his ship," Ngiraklsong says. "And you don't sail away from home with any captain."

Clouds move in from the east, a line of rain that deletes neighboring islands, erases the horizon. Never mind. Brilliant as these places are, they are broiling in the middle of the day. While other visitors scurry off, Ngiraklsong and I take refuge under a tin-roofed shelter, eat some turkey sandwiches from Winchell's Donuts, fall into easy conversation and relaxed silence. Ngiraklsong tells me about a retired policeman he recently visited in Atlanta, Georgia. The man had spent just six months in Palau, back in 1946, and he remembered everything. Palau has that way of imprinting itself, heightening memory, as if something decides without your knowing it that these days, these places and faces, are all keepers.

On the way back to Koror we move in and out of squalls. It's hard to talk. There's a part of the story of Wilson and Lee Boo, part of the story that the Palauans leave out. It's about Madan Blanchard, an ordinary seaman who stayed behind in Palau while Lee Boo sailed off to England. "I want to know why you stayed behind when the others went," E.M. Forster wrote in "A Letter to Madan Blanchard." Blanchard was a youth, illiterate and unremarkable. "Like any other seaman at £2 a month, good tempered, inoffensive, quiet, enjoyed fighting — the usual thing." A century and a half after the fact, Forster wondered about Blanchard. "The ends of the earth, the depths of the sea, the darkness of time, you have chosen all three." Forster speculated that the heady experience of inter-island warfare turned Blanchard's head. Given two wives at the start, he must have felt like a golden boy, for awhile, before the muskets grew rusty or the ammunition ran low, before his demands escalated and his presence grew tiresome. "He became arrogant and licentious, as persons are apt to do, when suddenly raised to unusual power and consequences," according to Amasa Delano, an American sea captain who called at Palau a few years afterward. Blanchard and a handful of followers had been ambushed and put to death. A Palauan prince dies and is mourned in London, an ordinary seaman dies an obscure death in Palau. A lesson's there, and a warning.

Johnson Toribiong and I sit at dinner at a hotel that overlooks Koror. We can see the blinking red lights at the airport, traffic moving along the main road, called Topside since Navy times, and turning west we can see causeways connecting Koror with Arakebesan and Malakai. I've known Toribiong for years, since he returned from school in the States, saw him leading Palau's secession from Micronesia. Back in Palau, where he now runs a law firm, serves as ambassador to Taiwan, and owns an apartment building, Toribiong and his partner began our "Togoland" dinners, named after one of the first international trusteeships — a League of Nations mandate — to be terminated. Palau was the last. The Togoland dinners involved beer, wine, cognac, steaks and potatoes, anecdote and speculation. A high-ranking Palauan, twice a presidential candidate, Toribiong enjoys the conversations of outsiders who are not strangers. But tonight Toribiong's schedule is tight. I quickly tell Johnson that I have divided recent Palauan history into periods. The first period is the Age of Blood. Blood refers to the capture of Palau from the Japanese, the destruction of the stylish colonial city the Japanese had built, its shops and arcades, stately residences and temples. The Japanese colonists far outnumbered the Palauans, who sometimes admit that they were a generation or so from being absorbed by Japan. The battles on Peleliu and Angaur ended that era, though veterans kept returning, heading down to Peleliu for a last look at Orange Beach and Bloody Nose Ridge. The Japanese didn't forget either, but when they returned they came as investors. Palau and the persistence of memory: the time you spend there gets separated out, like gold from sand, from the rest of your life.

The Age of Beer comes next. Toribiong listens closely, amused. The Age of Beer is where I came in. The mid-sixties. The beer was Kirin, Asahi, Olympia, Budweiser — all captured the market at different times, though Bud is king today. Back then, beer was cheap: five dollars could take you on a bobsled ride of an evening, especially on those twice monthly Fridays when Trust Territory government employees pissed away their earnings in lip-loosening and Walpurgisnachts that tracked through a half dozen waterside bars and ended at dawn on one of the old seaplane ramps that sloped down into the water off Arakebesan Island. Beer was beer alright, the currency of the realm, whole pallets of it lovingly unloaded and neatly stacked while household furniture, school supplies, government equipment suffered in heat and rain. Beer was also garbage. Crushed, discarded cans epitomized the dented, rusted, leaking Koror of that era, when water shortages and power outages made it feel like one of those poignant, left behind loser towns you listen to in country western music. A legacy of Navy times, country music was popular and its plangent lyrics fit the place. "Behind Closed Doors," "Am I So Easy to Forget" and "Please Release Me" were national anthems. The Age of Beer was a congenial time, static, even torpid, but garnished with excitement about what was to come. People were starting to picture the end of the United States trusteeship, wondering aloud about independence. A nation-building time was coming and I got to know some of the putative fathers of the country well, a moody charismatic Palauan, Lazarus Salii best of all. Towards the end of my Peace Corps service, I wrote speeches and press releases for Salii. I was his Sorenson, he was my Kennedy. Something like that. My Peace Corps days were over. I'd returned to the U.S., where I worked as a newspaperman for the Wall Street Journal, in its Los Angeles bureau: that was but a half life. My heart was in the islands, where a new age was rolling in: the Age of Bullshit, reaching from the late '60s into the mid '80s. Bombast, braggadocio, bravura, I considered them all but in the end I came back to Bullshit. Bullshit isn't all bad and sometimes isn't bad at all. Bullshit is highly charged exchange, playful colloquy, elegant speech. Also, self-serving nonsense. Bullshit is a matter of relative emphasis. There was still beer around. And blood, too.

The short history of those years is that Palau separated itself from the rest of the old Trust Territory — the northern Marianas, the Marshalls, the eastern Carolines — and cut a deal with the United States, a relationship of "free association," in which the new Republic of Palau would have sovereign, self-governing power and, in exchange for fifteen years of financial aid, would grant the United States military rights and foreign affairs authority. That the compact of free association led to a decade of turbulence, the murder of Palau's first elected president and the likely suicide of its second, my friend Lazarus Salii, has nothing to do with the idea of free association. It's what was always in the cards. My hunch is that anyone who thought otherwise, who mentioned independence, was kidding themselves or someone else. The Palauan ordeal was intramural: litigation, arson, murder, strikes, riots, eight bitter elections before the deal with the Americans was approved. It was Palauans against Palauans. The nature of the government wasn't at stake, it was who would run it, who would control the funds that came in. Too many people were in competition, Palauans who'd been on-island all along, Palauans returning from Trust Territory jobs in Saipan, a huge cast of players, focusing their energy on Palau, crowding each other out. Doctoral theses, books, articles, lawsuits detail those years, but despite all the writing, this is one of those situations that time will not heal, that history will not sort out. I can't imagine a full fair accounting from an outsider, who would miss things, or from a Palauan, who would be too close. What it came to was that there was more ambition, more dreaming, more greed than a small group of islands could accommodate.

So here I am, sitting across from Johnson Toribiong at our Togoland V dinner and, now that I have finished with the Age of Blood, Age of Beer, Age of Bullshit, I give him my impressions of the Palau I've encountered on this trip. I need to be fair: I am talking about a place I care about and I run all the risks of an outsider offering a comment. I'm not a Palauan, I don't speak more than scraps of the language, I don't live here, vote, pay taxes, invest money. I admit all this, admit that everyone who lives here knows more about Palau than I do, except for one thing: how they look to me. And this is something that Palauans help me discover: what is this the Age of!

"I'm worried," says Haruo Willter, sitting in an office on the third floor of the Ben Franklin store. The place is jammed with long rows of filing cabinets, storage boxes, office furniture; these are all that's left of the Trust Territory government and Willter is its last representative, a long-time employee of the U.S. Department of Interior. He is a man who turns out the lights. And he's worried about what has replaced the Trust Territory, a Republic of Palau whose government costs between $50-$60 million per year but raises about $30 million in taxes. The fifteen-year compact with the U.S. ends in 2009, but the Republic has already spent allocations through 2007. A separate U.S.-endowed trust fund may buy a few more years but Willter feels that Palau has a government it cannot sustain, not just a costly national government but sixteen state governments as well, each with a governor, a legislator, and its own license plates. Sooner or later, the Republic will need more money. And its pleas for aid may not be persuasive. Willter recalls what a skeptical visitor told him. "You need money, you're asking for it," the visitor said. "But individually, you're doing well. You put your beer and soda in a $300 cooler and your $32,000 4x4 vehicle, drive down to the dock, get in your $10,000, 200 horsepower boat and you go to the Rock Islands and drink beer and it just doesn't add up."

I drive with editor-publisher Moses Uludong through the streets of Koror. Sometimes it seems we have been meeting here forever. Twenty-five years ago, he read and hated my first novel, *The Day That I Die.* He decided to beat me up, at least give me a hard time. He came up to me in a bar called the Peleliu Club and escorted me outside, where a number of his pals were waiting for me, leaning against the back of a pick-up truck. The night was starry, the music was loud, the lot had potholes and we all had a lot to drink. Moses complained about the less-than-noble portrayal of Palauans in my steamy thriller, demanded to know who was the model for this or that character. I think he suspected he was in it. I went on about fictional characters, willful suspension of disbelief, the story's not true but there's truth in it. The proceedings sputtered out and we've been friendly ever since. Now we look back, sighing, on days when people worried about what the Americans would do to Palau, conspiracies about military bases, speculation about spies and CIA agents — I was on the list of suspects — dossiers and hidden agendas. Now we see yesterday's victims turned into today's exploiters, prospering as importers of foreign labor, raffling off their patrimony on a deal-by-deal basis, as if the proof of their sovereignty was their ability to sell off and out. The same money making schemes pop up year after year, free trade zones, super ports, casinos, garment factories, hotels, new airports, and they all have one element in common: Palauans don't work in them.

Moses and I drive along Topside, aiming to spend a day on Babeldaob. Two Filipino workers ride in back; they'll spend the day enlarging the cooking area in Moses' relatives' house. Traffic is slow. Moses says there are 16,000 cars in Palau now, fifty to eighty new ones coming in every month, two or three in front of every house. There's trouble coming, Moses senses, a loss of drive, ability, even language skills in the younger generation. What we're in now is the lull before the storm. Palau has six thousand foreign workers, mostly Filipinos, an increasing number of Chinese, plus Sri Lankans, Bangladeshis, Nepalese and, just lately, Russians, four prostitutes who set up in a nightclub on the edge of the mangroves in Airai. "Guys were selling their fish and then spending $100 to be with a white woman," Moses tells me. By the time deportation orders found them, three of the four women had married Palauans.

"There's a relation between the size of a population, the size of the government, the size of the private sector," a local businessman tells me. "And the fact that they've been out of balance for fifty years doesn't mean they won't have to pay up eventually. And no one wants to have that conversation." We're sitting in an all-but-empty dining room of a hotel placed, or misplaced, on Topside, overlooking a sea of rust-roofed neighboring houses. Nearer by, the swimming pool has collapsed, turning into a fenced-off mud-colored catch basin. Once-white walls are dappled by flecks of blackish mold: I'm told the contractor failed to mix an anti-fungal agent into the paint. Built by the investment arm of Taiwan's Kuomintang party, the hotel is now rumored to be for sale.

"It's cheaper to hire a foreign college graduate than a Palauan with a high school degree," the businessman tells me. That's the problem. What are Palauans going to do? They aren't going to fish for a living. Oh, they'll fish alright, fish passionately, but not commercially, not on those wretched fishing boats that go out beyond the reef for weeks on end. Nor will they farm; they'll hire foreign workers to work their land. What they will do is work for the Republic of Palau. And that brings me to what I hear from one of my oldest friends, a sometime businessman, sometime politician, named Polycarp Basilius.

"Face reality," Polycarp tells me. "Let all Palauans work for the government so they get their fair share of the money, benefits, insurance, security. Work for the government and let the private sector be done by foreigners. Government work is no sweat, no work; a guaranteed salary every two weeks. Play sports, work for the government, wait for the national elections."

What a formula! America finances the government, business is open to investors from the Pacific and Asia, Palauans sit at desks and talk. And talk. The coffee shop where Polycarp and I sit is one of a half dozen places where officials and politicians converge each morning, chewing betelnut, drinking endless cups of coffee served by Filipino waitresses. At Furasato, Penthouse, Rock Islands Cafe, it's the weekday morning talk show, conversations across the room, table to table, sports and weather, baiting and teasing that goes for hours and even longer during water shortages, when restaurant toilets flush while others falter. Don't get me wrong. I love the pleasure Palauans take in talking to each other; I love the web of news and rumor that they endlessly spin. "They're like birds on a wire," a friend told me, "squawking and shitting all day long." How long, I wonder, can they go on like this? The question haunts me as I make my way through Koror, haphazardly transformed from the rickety, bullet-pocked postwar place I remember, crowded now with cars, gas stations, bars, taxi stands, apartments, hotels half-empty, hotels half built, so it's hard to say whether they are going up or coming down. "If you build it, they will come" isn't the slogan here. No, it is: "If they pay for it, you will build it."

This is a time when Palau must provide for its future, this is when the Republic needs to make money. But making money is not the same as taking money, which is what they are doing now, taking money from the United States, Japan, Taiwan, Korea, from governments and private investors. And sometimes this place, which can feel like the heart of the world, turns into the ass-end of creation and my dream of island life turns into a nightmare of no escape. Suddenly, Forster's words to Madan Blanchard mock me: "The ends of the earth, the depths of the sea, the darkness of time, you have chosen all three." I see my imaginary front porch damp and creaking, termites chewing, rejection slips reaching me from New York, my imaginary Palauan wife wondering why we stay in this place when we could be living in Guam and it is dawning on both of us that our union is — and always was — heading in separate directions, she outward bound and me looking for island roots. Not that people don't know me here. My marriage to a Palauan woman has involved me in a net of traditional obligations, "custom" in English shorthand, ocheraol in Palauan, which means that I'm expected to donate food, beer or cash when a relative — and believe me, everyone is related — is born, marries, dies, or builds a house. Custom is one of the things that holds Palau together, I am told. It also manages to pick me clean: about $4,000 a year these days and the more I make, the more I'll be asked for. I'll never get even. Interestingly, more than half the Palauans who leave Palau list escape from customary obligations as a reason for their departure. The local Palauan population stays static for a reason. So does my flat-line savings account. I may never get out; there'd be a gamut of un- or little-known relatives at the airport, an expression of sullen entitlement on their faces. The life I picture gets further away all the time. I'm not a novelist, I'm a character in a novel, unpublished, unpublishable...

"I was a Trust Territory kid," says Margo Vitarelli, "raised on Guam, Saipan and Palau. I went swimming in my underwear at M dock. I paddled in a canoe made out of roofing tin." I find her at the Palau Museum, which sits on a breezy knoll that lifts out of the man groves on the backside of Koror. Margo's life, like my own, has several Palauan chapters, including childhood, marriage to a Palauan man, employment in education and, just lately, at the Palau Museum. Like me, she's kept coming back. I ask why.

"There's the ocean itself," she says, "the water that's so warm, so clear, so flat. In Hawaii, the waves are freezing cold, uninviting. It was food and boats and friends, going to the Rock Islands. It was the rooted sense of a small town, knowing everybody. Those conversations across a room — everything comfortable, relaxing, secure..." Her voice trails off. She laughs a little, then resumes. "Predictable. Boring."

She's leaving to marry a lawyer in Virginia. He has no connection to Palau and when he came to the island that meant so much to her, the magic escaped him. "I saw the place as it appears to someone who has no history here, no knowledge of the past," she recalls. "He kept asking, 'why don't they?' — 'Why don't they re-design Koror, if they want to turn it into Bermuda?' And 'Why don't they redesign the legal system? Why don't they have building codes, if tourism is the goal? Why don't they pave that road? Fill that pothole? How can they cut those trees?'" She wonders, as I do, whether people coming to Palau now will fall in love with it the way we once did. Oh, there are plenty of newcomers, lawyers on two-year contracts, diving in their spare time, moving on. That's not the kind of connection that lasts a lifetime.

"People arriving today cannot hang out with Palauans the way we did," Margo suspects. "They can't learn the beauty, the passion and humor of Palauans, can't see beneath the surface. They're puzzled. They wonder, why did I come here? Why did I stay so long?"

Leaving the museum, I see a traditional Palauan abai, with the legends of the race carved into panels on the sides of the thatch-roofed building. There's a pile of World War II weapons and a statue of Palau's assassinated first president, Haruo Remeliik. A two minute downhill drive takes me to the Koror Jail, where the man convicted of ordering Remeliik's death is serving a life sentence. I linger in the front office, where the wall is covered with story boards resembling what I have just seen at the museum's abai. These are carved by prisoners, sold to tourists. It's not my first visit. I return again because of a small favor, a long time ago. As a Peace Corps volunteer, I was stranded in a Palauan bar at Saipan at closing time, five miles from home. I didn't have a car. The Peace Corps liked volunteers to walk; they still believed that voluntary poverty impressed people. Eventually, after some consultation at the other end of the bar, a Palauan invited me into his car and towards the end of our early morning ride, introduced himself: John O. Ngiraked, a Senator in the Congress of Micronesia, a traditional leader and, I later learned, one of the most eloquent speakers of the Palauan language. Ngiraked's later career had its ups and downs. He was the Republic's Foreign Minister for a while but the highest posts went to other men, and the biggest business deals. He brought a well-worn ship — nicknamed the Love Boat — to Palau, hoping it would prosper as an entertainment center. Haruo Remeliik's government condemned it as an environmental menace. In prison for ordering the president's death, Ngiraked still contends that the government owes him $500,000 for his lost vessel. He displays little hope of collecting the money, or for that matter, of walking out of prison anytime soon.

Conversation is the measure of life and death in Palau, it conjugates past, present, and future. You don't just walk in, ask a question and walk away. This is especially, and understandably, the case with John Ngiraked. Still carrying an air of importance, he guides me to a wooden bench in a puddled inside courtyard. He talks of his health, his reading, his writing — an ungainly, self-published history of Palau — and a new project which will be a collection of his correspondence with famous people. He talks of his life in prison, his faith in God. And, summoning up some of the eloquence I remember, he tells me what he makes of these days in Palau, the current affluence and underlying angst.

"We are going through a quiet kind of decline, an ambiance of confusion and chaos," he says. "All these foreign workers are a good and bad thing. Palau is saturated with English in government and with Tagalog from Filipino nannies at home. A car is broken, a simple appliance needs fixing, a Filipino guy is there. The good part is it's cheap labor. But, in its consequences, it's not cheap. We are paying dearly. Look around. Walk the streets. Where are you? You can't tell." If John Ngiraked is Palau's fallen leader, Noah Idechong is its young defender, winner of the Goldman Foundation environmental award. I meet him just across the road from the jail at a cyberspace cafe that sells Starbucks Coffee. "The more I work on the environment," he tells me, "the more I see that the environment is a symptom of other things. We're losing our Palauan stock, an overall loss of connection to the land, to the islands, to nature... that special relationship, the sort of thing that, wherever you are, makes you want to come back here because this is where you belong."

So there I am, having pasta and wine at Togoland V, facing Johnson Toribiong, summarizing these conversations, high and low, wondering aloud about these best and worst of times, this government sometimes mendicant, sometimes arrogant, worried about the place and knowing that some people would argue I haven't the right to worry at all.

"Palauans don't work enough," Toribiong says. "We drive a car, drink coffee, read newspapers and call it work." When Toribiong pauses, I recall a visit up the coast of Babeldaob where a guy was snoozing under a palm tree in the middle of the day. "People come from all around the world to be on our beaches," he maintained. "Me, I live here. I can do it every day," he said. Now, back to Toribiong. "This," he says, "is the Age of the Barbecue."

To relieve crowding in Koror, to open up the sparsely populated island of Babeldaob, to celebrate its birth as a new nation, with embassies in Washington and Tokyo and at the United Nations, the Republic of Palau is building a new capitol. I am urged to see it and, as it turns out, I see it twice. Once would have been enough: it's an hour and a half long, axle-busting, bladder-splitting ride on washed out red clay roads. My first trip is with Moses Uludong who thinks the whole idea of a new capitol is a mistake. Then, Polycarp Basilius decides to take me on the same trip. Once again I find myself crossing the Japanese-donated bridge that links Koror and Babeldaob, bouncing north through three or four of the Republic's sixteen states. We cross and recross a new round-the-island highway, a $140 million road paid for by the United States, constructed by a Korean firm employing Filipino and Indonesian workers. More than half-finished, the road will link villages previously reached by boats. Environmentalist Noah Idechong thinks the new road is Palau's top environmental threat. He foresees a laissez-faire land rush, bulldozer propelled, with mangroves, lagoons and reef paying the price. "The opportunity to screw up will be big," he warns. That doesn't bother the man who's taking me to the capitol this morning. For years, Polycarp Basilius has mocked my feeling for the environment, especially my concern for the Rock Islands. "I'm going to knock down those islands," he promises. "Use them to make roads. Maybe we'll keep one island for people to see. The rest we'll quarry." A cheerful predator, Polycarp likes action. Though he often got elected to the old Congress of Micronesia, he left big issues — political status — to others. He was more of a local interests guy, sometimes very local. A showy advertisement in the Palau yellow pages features one of his mansions, a pink Romanesque place in Melekeok that has a statue of a nude Olympic discus thrower poised upon the arch of his driveway. Below this picture comes a list of Polycarp's various enterprises, from shipping, construction and insurance to a duck farm. Not all of Polycarp's big deals have come off yet. He was involved in a controversial oil super port proposal that died. He still talks of offshore oil drilling. Now he confides his plans to build an elite Catholic University of Palau in the hills of Babeldaob. My hints that this project is out of scale, that Palau already has a likable community college, that a population of 20,000 cannot sustain a university, that almost all students would be on scholarship, that a university in Palau might be a university or might be Palauan, but could not be both, do not deter him. "It'll happen," he assures me. "It's a done deal." Meanwhile, there's the new capitol.

"The architect proposed something that was Pacific Island style," Polycarp tells me. "And something else that was

Hawaiian style. I told him, 'I like Washington.'" Washington it is. Washington on a tiny island, Washington for the population of a midwestern county seat, Washington built by foreign labor, mostly financed by the government of Taiwan. There's a round presidential office attached to an executive office. The legislature and judiciary, now jammed into old Japanese buildings in Koror, are grandly situated in air-conditioned buildings with sealed windows and daunting columns. A dome will raise the legislature to the height of an eleven-story building. As soon as I see the place I know that these buildings will be commented on for years, a field day for enthusiasts, a feast for ironists. And a lesson for me. All the time I was picturing Palau from half a world away, Palau was looking back, looking at America. This capitol, this tribute and mockery, obliterates the bracing distance between us.

"The Spanish came for God, the Germans for glory, the Japanese came for gold, the Americans came for good." That's an old saying about these islands that I had wanted to avoid repeating but the new capitol makes it irresistible. Americans came for good: permanence and benevolence combining. At the heart of the magic of small islands, especially small Pacific islands that were the last places in the world to secure their independence, was the hope that they would benefit from the rest of the world's mistakes. Perhaps it had to be. Now I wonder whether, if we looked at these islands from a distant star, we might be able to detect the moment when this Washington-on-Melekeok became inevitable, something that happened a long time ago that changed everything, that meant the ballgame I played was over before it began. Was it the firearms that Madan Blanchard and his shipmates carried up the coast of Babeldaob? Was it the first mass, the first movie, the first cold beer? The first — the first thousand — foreign workers?

"Palau is no threat to the world," I write on my last day. "But the world is a threat to Palau, not by design, not intentionally, but accidentally. Nature abhorring a vacuum." The world will come at the Palauans, who will conspire in their own undoing. All the cynicism in the world, all the naïveté will not protect them. And yet, I will keep returning, because there is too much that I value here. I still can find some of the old Palauan cockiness and pride of self. I see it in bright eyed sassy school kids — one hopes that there will be better things for them to do than boss foreign workers around — and in the steely, measuring eyes of old timers, wise and unapologetic. I hear it in the Palauan language that I love the sound of; though I don't know a sentence, I hear it in my dreams, crackling from table to table in the morning, traveling — like radio waves — further at night. I love the way all Palauans, in nouveau riche mansions or in haphazard wood and-tin shacks, have a place, a shed or lean-to, where they sit out of doors, napping, cooking and washing, talking way into the night. I love the interest they take in each other, the time that they spend, the wave and weave of life. "Every morning I get up and look around and I say thankyou, thankyou, thankyou," says one American who lives here. I feel thankful too. Those things that Forster wrote of, "the ends of the earth, the depths of the sea, the darkness of time," don't work anymore. The succoring, simplifying dream of islands is over. But this won't stop me from thinking about Palau. Sad story, same old story, it doesn't matter. I will find myself picturing the place, feeling a time of day, a tone of voice, a snatch of music, a certain walk and attitude. I will spin the globe, running my fingers over all the places I ought to see. And I will go back to the place where I've already been, to find out how my life is turning out.

Remembering Saipan

Antioch Review, Winter 2005

Five hours out of Los Angeles, another seven west of Hawaii — twelve hours of cramped seats and crap food — and now, headed north from Guam, the weariness and claustrophobia depart. I enter a zone of magic, a field of force. The island of Saipan, haunted, handsome, out-of-control Saipan, awaits me, just twenty minutes away. We'll be landing at night but I can picture the place anytime, its beaches and caves, the mountain at its center, the fatal cliffs. Island of dreams and nightmares for me and, even more, for the men I am traveling with, two dozen World War II veterans, some accompanied by wives, a few by sons, and at least one, late actor Lee Marvin, represented by his widow. The greatest generation, they've been called, here to mark the sixtieth anniversary of the Battle of Saipan.

I first glimpse them at an airport hotel in Los Angeles, men of a certain age, out of place among younger travelers who are watching the Lakers duel the Pistons and enjoying fajitas and Corona beers at a hotel bar. The old-timers dutifully display their name tags, "Military Historical Tours." For the next fifteen hours, in airport vans and departure lounges, standing in aisles, loitering outside airplane restrooms, I chat and eavesdrop as we travel across time zones and datelines. What I hear at first is random, tentative. How could it be otherwise? One man talks about the discovery of a cache of Japanese saki in the ruins of Saipan' s town of Garapan, another recalls the taste of beer turned skunky in the island's withering heat. A pilot remembers some buddies who built a jeep out of spare parts, just for the fun of it. When ordered to tum the vehicle in, they drove it to a cliff and pushed it into the same waters where Japanese soldiers and civilians jumped to their deaths months before. Another veteran swears he wants to eat barracuda, yet another — a Kansas farmer — longs to find the place where he was shot. There's a deeper vein of memory, I guess, but what comes first are careful, practiced things they've said before. Memories on command. I wonder when — or if — I will hear memories that show up without permission. Still, I like them. They are old, there's no getting away from it. I hear talk of macular degeneration's attack on vision, of impending heart surgery, of hip replacements past and planned.

Sixty years ago, death was dispensed on Saipan from ships, aircraft, artillery, tanks, machine guns, flamethrowers, grenades, rifles, pistols, bayonets, swords, bamboo spears, clubs, stones, and fists. Now, for the men sitting in the darkened cabin of this plane, death is subtler, gradual. It assaults their knees and hips, congests their hearts, clouds their eyes, clogs their ears. The battle — their victory — cost more than 3,000 American lives, but that was a fraction of the 70,000 Americans who attacked and took the island. The odds were in their favor then. Not now. Watching them fly halfway around the world after sixty years, seeing them nap, stare at movies, pick at food, I find myself pleased to accompany them on this last long journey.

"Reason for trip," one veteran muses as he reads from a form the stewardess passes out between Guam and Saipan. The Commonwealth of the Northern Marianas wants to know why we are coming. Business or pleasure? Employment? Visit relatives? Reason for trip: a battle that history's neglected. We've had a week of D-Day and Normandy,

Saving Private Ryan stuff. But, by bringing Japan in range of B-29s with atomic bombs, the capture of Tinian and Saipan ended World War II. Reason for visit? The veteran checks off "a previous trip." That'll do for him. And for me.

Back in 1967, the Peace Corps announced — half kiddingly — that it was going to "paradise." That was Micronesia, a U.S.-administered United Nations Trusteeship which covered the northern Marianas, including Saipan and Tinian, as well as the distant, scattered, Caroline and Marshall Islands. I didn't ask for paradise. I'd been reading Lawrence Durrell, not James Michener. Picturing labyrinthine cities, spicy, crowded marketplaces, exotic and dangerous liaisons, I specified Turkey and Ethiopia. But the Peace Corps tapped me for paradise. Someone I never met changed my life forever. And saddled me with a mantra that I learned, memorized, recited, and wrote, then and for years to come: "The Trust Territory of Pacific Islands has 2,141 islands with an aggregate land mass half the size of Rhode Island scattered over an area the size of the continental United States. And a population of 120,000 that could be — possibly — accommodated in the Pasadena Rose Bowl. It has six districts, nine mutually-unintelligible languages, and a subsistence economy of fishing and farming as well as the copra trade, scrap metal, and government employment." Sometimes, if my listeners' eyes weren't glazing over, I would add that this was the last post-World War II trusteeship and that America was supposed to offer the people a choice of their future government and political status. Eventually, sort of, somehow, maybe… Oh, there was no escaping it, I had been sent to a place that not many people cared about, a few pieces of small change jangling around in history's pocket. But that didn't stop me from falling in love.

The Saipan I came to was no paradise, that was clear. Almost a quarter century had passed since the shooting stopped, but the place was shaped and defined by the great battle. Long after the military walked away from its quonsets, camps, and airfields, the island was haunted. It was like a theater abandoned by actors and audience, a place still littered with costumes and props, ticket stubs and programs. Have you ever, driving around America, gone past an outdoor drive-in theater, the big screen still standing, blank as death, weeds in the parking lot, long half-circular rows of those speakers that look like parking meter poles, and the ruins of a rickety, graffiti-marked projection booth in the middle of it all? That was Saipan. It had battlefield beaches, rusting tanks and landing craft, bullet-pocked Japanese buildings, abandoned runways, houses cobbled together out of left-behind wood and scavenged metal. Saipan was one of those rare, dear places where you could confront history without a ticket, a tape-recorded spiel, a forced march through a museum, a sign at the entrance warning of all the things you weren't supposed to do. That was Saipan, all right, scarred, handsome, and sometimes at the right time of day, beautiful. It invited exploring, it conduced to thought. It kept me — it keeps me — coming back, an ex-Peace Corps Volunteer among ex-Marines. So, reason for visit? "A previous trip."

Night on Saipan greets me like an intimate friend, that heavy, velvety, not-quite-liquid air that wraps itself around me as I step through the terminal. The veterans take their time, wait for luggage. My stuff is hand-carried and I move fast, wanting to be all the way home. That "I have returned" business can be very impressive, I tell myself, a minute before I feel like a fool. As I step through the terminal, first off the plane, I draw cheers and shouted "thank yous." No, I need to protest, I wasn't here in the battle. I was a Peace Corps Volunteer here in the late sixties, I've written about the place in magazines and books, but no... I'm not one of them. Embarrassed, furtive, I brush aside an interview request: "Peace Corps, not Marine Corps," I confess.

I sit out on the balcony of the Hyatt Hotel. I'm worried. I almost didn't come. An old friend thought I might have something interesting to say. He pressed for my invitation — a plane ticket and a hotel room in exchange for a speech. Others were skeptical: I was not a veteran, not a military historian. What did I have to talk about? "Saipan from Then to Now" became my topic, an account of the island from the end of the war, through years of United States Trusteeship, all the way to its current status as a United States Commonwealth. It's a tricky subject and my problem is that I'll be facing two incompatible audiences. There are veterans who will want something celebratory. Fair enough. But there'll be others, Saipan residents, who want to know what I make of today's bewildering island. What to do? It's a predicament. Amazing, what you can get yourself into when you care about small places. Still, there's this: from my balcony, with the sliding door open behind me, I straddle two climates, air conditioning at my back, tropical night in front. It's wasteful and delicious.

Down below, I survey a honeymoon landscape: irregularly shaped swimming pools set among banks of succulent plants and tropical trees through which young Japanese wander on floodlit paths, heading for a beachside dance pavilion where a band is playing "By the Waters of Babylon," set to an easy-to-dance-to cha-cha beat. That hasn't changed, at least: all dances around here are cha-chas. And they go on forever, turning a potential romantic encounter into a punitive work-out exercise, with one song so quickly followed by another, similar song that it's hard to exit the floor without feeling defeated. Still, there's something rich and plangent about music coming to you through the warm night. Behind the pools and pavilion lies the Philippine Sea, dark and neglected feeling, except for the lights on offshore ships. Three of those ships are almost always there. They're pre-positioned U.S.-chartered military supply ships, "beans and bullets" set to sail to trouble spots on a moment's notice. That's today's Saipan, living off continuing U.S. military interest, off Japanese tourists, off a couple of dozen garment factories where foreign workers — Chinese mainly — make clothing marked American-made. There were 11,000 people, mostly local, when I came here in the 1960s; now there are more than 70,000, mostly foreign: garment makers, security guards, barbers and beauticians, hostesses and maids, farmers and hard-hats who have come to do the island's heavy lifting. The Saipanese work mostly for the island government. It's a scrap of America. I wonder what the veterans will make of it. I wonder what I make of it.

It howled irony when I first heard that Saipan's neighbor island of Tinian would become home to a Chinese-financed casino. The casino at the end of the world, that's how I thought of it. A casino on the A-bomb island, the place the Enola Gay called home. Why not Tarawa for high-rollers, why not Pitcairn or St. Helena? Now, on almost the first day of my return, I join the veterans on a casino-operated hydrofoil that shuttles the few miles between Saipan and Tinian. When we arrive, after a welcoming ceremony at the dock, we bundle into a van and head to a Japanese peace monument at the far end of the island. After lunch at the casino, veterans mingling with indifferent gamblers at buffet tables, we head to the main attraction: the north end of the island, where 8,500-foot airstrips are baking in afternoon heat, surrounded by brushy boondocks that give off the smell of steamed green vegetables. I prefer the runways on moonlit nights, when I have them to myself, and go racing down the runway in a rental car, headlights dimmed, right on the edge of history. Today, the heat is awful, yet veterans step out onto the runways, return to the van, step back out at the pits from which atomic bombs were hoisted aboard the Enola Gay and its companion plane, Bockscar. This is where the war ended and the atomic age began, and the emptiness of the place is startling: big sky, heat-waved breezes blowing down the endless runway. At last, with lots of time to kill, we find some shade on the tiny, lightly-defended beaches where the invasion surprised the Japanese. I can't come here without thinking about the Japanese garrison. What did it feel like to see 500 ships converging on Saipan, to see the better-manned island go up in smoke, to measure the progress of a losing battle, off the beaches, toward the mountain, then to Suicide and Banzai Cliffs? What was it like for the Japanese on Tinian to know not only that they were doomed but also that their last battle was a sideshow, nine days of fighting that cost about 300 American lives and 8,000 Japanese? For the Americans, it was as close to perfect as a battle can be. But, as I idle away an afternoon with the victors, I wonder about their doomed opponents. Was their greatness any less than that of the "greatest generation"? If greatness means courage, they surely had it. And loyalty? Yes, to a fault. Willingness to sacrifice for king and country? The numbers speak for themselves. Should we grant them greatness, then? If not, on what grounds do we deny it? And did one side — our side — require a greatness in its opponents? Did they need each other? The way Joe Louis needed Max Schmeling?

There's a pillbox on the invasion beach, one of countless such fortifications all through Micronesia, damp, pock-marked places, moldy and garbage-littered within, pissed-in and picked-over. The highest-ranking member of our group, a retired three-star general, is standing near the pillbox. I ask him how such stolid, ugly structures were attacked. Throw a hand grenade through the firing slot, when you can get close enough, he replies. Or use a flame thrower. Shooting into the mouth of the cave like a fatal French kiss, the napalm tongue burns the men inside or, by sucking out all the air, suffocates them. And like that, a fort becomes a tomb. And once again, I wonder about the other side, the underdogs, the lost cause, history's villains and Hollywood's as well. Would a gathering of eighty-year-old Germans or Japanese be that much different?

Late-afternoon shadows cross the beach, the killing heat begins to abate, the day turns mellow. I fall into conversation with Hal Olsen. He had a career at Los Alamos, an artist-illustrator for the government. Lots of work, he says, was classified. Back here, he's enjoying a late flush of fame as a nose-cone artist. He's one of the men who painted women on the front of B-29s flying out of Saipan and Tinian, languorous, seductive pin-up girls copied out of calendars and magazines. An odd trade and his work was perishable: he knows of only one example that still exists. But he has memories of bombers with names like Easy Maid and Lucky Lady. Up-and-Atem. His price was fifty dollars and he remembers standing on oil barrels while he painted, breathing coral dust stirred up by taxiing bombers, getting heckled by passing crews. "The nose-cone paintings were a touch of humanity," he says, "on what were otherwise killing machines."

The crowded, neon nightclub zone behind my hotel is Saipan's Ginza. By day it's dreary. In island humidity and heat, even the newest buildings age quickly. Mold rules. It's hard to say whether something has just been finished or is on the edge of demolition. We're talking about a warren of concrete buildings housing convenience stores, tourist shops, restaurants, night clubs, massage parlors, disco, karaoke, duty-free shopping. Look between the buildings and you see alleys of scrap lumber, ruptured bags of cement, hanging laundry, tangled wiring. But at night, no doubt about it, the place buzzes: teams of bar girls, Filipinas mostly, assemble outside nightclub entrances, dressed in uniform. It's as if the team in orange-sherbet-colored miniskirts is about to scrimmage against the squad across the street in Aqua Velva blue. Later, the masseuses come out, and they stay out a lot longer, chatting in chairs set out on the sidewalk, calling to, sometimes running across the street to connect with, passing customers. There are Russian women on the island now too: one place is called "Russian Roulette."

Tourism — about 500,000 visitors a year, mostly Japanese — is big business on Saipan, second only to the garment industry. The tourist era began back in the sixties, with just one oceanfront hotel that we were sure was doomed to fail. But soon there were hotels all up and down the invasion beach, almost all of them Japanese-owned and -patronized. That was the interesting thing: the pattern of tourist development mimicked the World War II battle. First they hit the beaches, then they moved inland to Mount Tagpochau, then north to Suicide and Banzai Cliffs. Hotels were trailed by camp-following, wake-of-battle operations: golf courses and shopping centers and poker machine parlors.

Who could have guessed — what ex-Marine, what ex-Peace Corps Volunteer — that Saipan would become a Japanese Florida? And what about the island's biggest industry, the garment trade, represented by factories and barracks across the island? Sometimes the labels specify the Commonwealth of the Northern Marianas, sometimes it's just Made in the U.S.A. Ten years ago, the garment operations were controversial. American labor unions objected, congressmen charged exploitation, TV and print journalists reported on workers living in shipping containers, dissidents shuttled off-island on night flights to Manila. Conditions have improved since then, I'm told, but the underlying situation continues to perplex. Take the benefits of living under the American flag, combine with influxes of foreign capital and foreign labor, retain control of local government, contact Washington when necessary, put them on hold when convenient, and prosper. It reminds me of Saudi Arabia, enriched by oil; of Nauru, which turned bat shit into gold. Saipan had location, location, location: the route that Colonel Tibbetts took north in the Enola Gay is the same route Japanese and Korean 747s now take, coming south.

What an island! What a confederacy of deals: of history and story, a newsreel battleground turned into a film noir. At night, headed to dinner with the veterans at the island's only major American-owned hotel, I pass through a neighborhood of garment factories. I drive carefully — I've been warned — because off-duty garment workers flit back and forth across the streets as if they were in Manila. Which they well might be. They've turned Saipan into Manila at night, with tiny ethnic stores, hole-in-the-wall currency-remittance operations, long distance phone centers. They've revived agriculture on the island: naked light bulbs dangle over tables full of eggplant, onions, greens, beans, avocados, garlic, melons, okra, com, soursop, kalamtsi. There are barbecue stands, smoke coming off pork, fish, chicken. Elsewhere, there are Korean restaurants, Chinese and Filipino, Indian and, a stone's throw from Saipan's Planet Hollywood, a tiny place called Taste of Bengla Desh. There's a Lower East Side immigrant buzz about Saipan, an accidental Ellis Island, even if most of these workers are fated to leave when their contracts end. Is all this the flush of growth or the phosphorescence of decay? Paradise? Paradise lost? Paradise leased? If you believe in island communities that are small, tightly woven, deeply rooted, what do you make of Saipan? If you believe in America as a level playing field, an equal-opportunity employer, something that offers the hope of time and work leading to membership and citizenship from the bottom up, how does Saipan measure up? One thing is certain: it's an island like no other.

After the Tinian tour, I have two days before the seminars and speeches begin. The veterans are being guided around Saipan, retracing the battle, so many Rip Van Winkles, matching memories of then with the reality of now. I go on my own search, looking for the island that hooked me in the sixties and never quite let go. Much of it is almost lost to factories, shopping centers, housing developments, some prospering, others shuttered, remnants of the fevered atmosphere that followed the island's becoming a Commonwealth. ("It's not the heat," someone quipped, "it's the cupidity.")

Still, even in the midst of what passes for progress, there are pockets of the past. Consider, for instance, Aslito, the Japanese precursor of today's busy international airport, where I meet an old friend, Jerry Facey, for an early morning walk. On this island, if you want to do anything physical, you get up at dawn. So we meet at six in the air cargo area, within sight of the main terminal and control tower. There are Japanese pillboxes and a few larger buildings in easy view: even the most casual tourist cannot miss them. But much more is waiting in the boondocks around the airport, buried in unwelcoming thickets of the brushy tangan-tangan plant that was seeded by air after the battle, to replace burned-off, never-to-be-replanted sugar cane fields. Quickly breaking a sweat, Facey and I walk down a maze of overgrown runways and bomber parking places ("hard stands") left by the Americans. Peeling back the layers of time, we tum into the tangan-tangan and find the ruins of a Japanese hospital: tiled floor, concrete sinks and cisterns, wards and waiting rooms. Elsewhere, there's an administration building, a power plant, an ammunition revetment: a Japanese colonial city, built to endure, handsome in its ruins.

No one visits here by accident. And there are places like this all over the island, waiting for anyone who cares enough to find them. Facey and I hop in his truck, drive down an axle-busting road, rocky and eroded, tangan-tangan leaning toward us from either side, branches swiping at our windows. We make our way toward Japanese artillery batteries facing toward Tinian, on Naftan point. They repose like Mayan ruins, tenanted by wasps and lizards. There's little reason for local people to come here, less for tourists: Hermes scarves, not rusted helmets, are today's souvenirs of Saipan. It's safe to say that no more than a dozen people have been here since the war, and equally few will come in the next twenty years.

Later, I go off on my own, headed toward Mount Tagpochau. On the road that cuts around the back side of the island, away from the invasion beaches, I find not houses but mansions; mini-Taras, some built by tax-avoiding American businessmen, others by Saipanese enriched by land leases. Still, the old ragged cliffs are here, the pocket beaches and blow holes, the windy fields of sawgrass, occasional breadfruit trees, ramshackle farms and pastureland, the island I remember. Battered in war, brutalized in peace, but still here. Next I drive north to Marpi, the wildest and emptiest part of the island. In my Peace Corps days, the place was off-limits; it was littered with unexpended live ammunition originally intended for the land invasion of Japan. The Saipanese used to sneak into the area fat night, harvesting scrap metal, bronze and copper fittings off live ammunition that sometimes exploded; hands and lives were lost. Later, Marpi attracted scavengers of another kind, Japanese bone-hunting missions retrieving remains of the war dead. They built a huge pyre on an old fighter strip down below Suicide Cliff. I saw rows upon rows of leg and arm bones, neatly piled like campfire logs, larger bones at the bottom, smaller on top and — at the very top — a row of skulls. Mission after mission came to the island and some people hinted that local guides were baiting caves with bones obtained from other places. After a while, the missions stopped. Saipanese worried that Japanese were intruding on local burial sites and there was a macabre rumor that someone got caught smuggling firearms in crates of remains headed to Japan from Saipan. Even if you passed up ammunition and bones, Marpi was a great place to wander. It had a rocky shoreline, shell-pocked cliffs, countless caves littered with mess kits, saki bottles, rubber boots, cooking pots. Many caves had been blasted shut with Japanese inside; with time, they were opening and you could crawl, if you wanted, into what amounted to a crypt.

On Suicide and Banzai Cliffs, at the end of the battle, Japanese, Koreans, Okinawans, soldiers and civilians, men, women, and children, enacted the largest mass suicide in history, at least until Reverend Jim Jones raised a Kool-Aid toast in Jonestown, Guyana. I've seen the Saipan jumpers in black-and-white newsreels, women leaping off cliffs into the sea, taking their children with them, even as Japanese-speakers with the American troops implored them to surrender. And, just this week, I heard something I can't get out of my mind: some people, I'm told, walked backwards off the cliffs, not wanting to know which step would be their last. That's an interesting choice. Here's another one: you could jump off Suicide Cliff, hundreds of feet high, landing on hard ground down below. But my choice, I guess, would be Banzai Cliff, a shorter fall into a turbulent rocky ocean, crashing waves, likely sharks and — what comes back to me now, when I revisit and sit awhile — the bluest possible sea, green-blue around rocks, light blue near the surface, and deep blue, cobalt blue, when it declines into the Marianas Trench, which is the deepest ocean anywhere.

In late afternoon, I find the road up to Saipan's peak, Mount Tagpochau. Halfway up, I come to the place where I worked as a Peace Corps Volunteer. "Mount Olympus," it was nicknamed back then, and it had a peculiar history. After World War II, all the islands we captured from the Japanese were made a United Nations Trusteeship. At first, the Navy administered the place. Then, in the early fifties, the U.S. Department of Interior took over. But not on Saipan, not for long. In no time, Saipan was returned to the Navy, almost certainly because it was the headquarters of an ultra-secret outfit called the Naval Technical Training Unit, or NTTU; "the secret place" was its local nickname, Mt. Tagpochau its home. For ten years, Saipan was off-limits to visitors and "the secret place" was off-limits to the United Nations Visiting Missions, who never glimpsed what was happening on the hill. What, then, were they up to? What I heard, when I arrived in 1967, was that they had been training Nationalist Chinese and also a darker-skinned group, possibly Indonesians, in infiltration, sabotage, and such. The NTTU students came in by the planeload, late at night, were shuttled through the gates in buses with blacked-out windows. This was a school that had no registrar, no alumni, no class reunions, no institutional memory. Except for this: every now and then, someone I knew on Saipan would tell me about a chance meeting with another American and — what a coincidence — they had a stay in Saipan in common: lovely place, no? But then, when the question arose, why were you on Saipan, when were you on Saipan, a curtain came down, the conversation ended. When I came to Saipan, all that was left of the NTTU were their houses and offices, an amazing California community, transplanted and tucked away on a hill overlooking the Pacific. The Trust Territory government had inherited the NTTU headquarters and what had been a hush-hush installation with the high commissioner — in 1967, a Hawaiian public relations man named Bill Norwood — living in the highest house. His subordinates, American and Micronesian, spread out below in dozens of rambling, airy concrete houses, typhoon-proof, with suburban driveways, well-barbered lawns, and a view that went miles and miles out into the Philippine Sea. It was an absurdity, a place-out-of-place, the setting for a comic opera or a Doonesbury cartoon, but Capitol Hill was nonetheless a kind of high-water mark of the American power that fought its way ashore on the Invasion beaches. It was bridge parties and cocktails and patios and good roads and a breezy hilltop at the end of the world. I was a Peace Corps Volunteer. I lived in a series of tin-roofed, wood-framed places with holes in the roof and the floor. That was where I belonged, they told me, on the level of the people. But the people I was living with looked up at this mini-America and decided they wanted Capitol Hill or something like it, maybe something better. And didn't that decision complete the conquest of Saipan? Now the governor of the U.S. Commonwealth of the Northern Marianas lives in the high commissioner's residence and the island is all-American. Happy endings all around, I suppose. But about a third of the houses on Capitol Hill are lived in, some of the rest limp along as minor government offices, and the rest are abandoned, boarded up, driveways cracked and littered with debris, lawns gone to weeds, and the whole place feels sad.

Next: two shrines. One is the Shrine of Lourdes, an inland cave where a number of islanders took shelter during the battle. They were lucky. Hundreds of other Saipanese perished. Tomorrow they will dedicate a monument to dead islanders: their names, engraved on a wall at the American Memorial Park, will be read aloud, one by one. There's a rumor that having long-gone relatives formally remembered acquired some cachet and people submitted the names of almost anyone who died on Saipan during the war, almost doubling the previous estimate: more than 900 names in all. In the end, though, people feel it doesn't hurt to err on the side of generosity. My Saipan shrine is Hamilton's Bar. On an island where nightlife is dominated by hot lights and loud music, by disco, karaoke, hostesses and masseuses, Hamilton's is one last link to the glorious nights of beer and bullshit I remember. All the other places are gone, those ramshackle places along Beach Road — Josie' s, Saipana, Apollo 11, Saipan Inn — where jukeboxes sent sad country-western tunes into the night and once you entered you were in for the duration, all the way until closing time, and there was no way of knowing how you'd get home. Peace Corps Volunteers weren't supposed to use cars. Never mind. In those days it was fun being stranded at a strange place at two in the morning, walking or waiting around or jumping in the back of a pick-up truck, headed out to a late-night restaurant for noodle soup or a nearby beach for more beer. It was all magic, back then. Saipan was still an island and you could tell yourself that no harm could come to you.

Hamilton's is the last place that feels that way. Its revered founder, Wilbur Hamilton, is buried outside but his presence hovers within. Each night, at nine p.m., the regulars — some Saipanese, some American — raise a glass in his memory. Hamilton was a Navy man, a country boy with a profane disregard for politicians, Peace Corps Volunteers, hustlers and geeks of all kinds, a hard-drinking, harmonica-playing bartender and bullshitter with a million stories and a good heart. He would have reveled in the conversation that goes on in his bar — war stories, con games, local politics — all garnished by mockery and humor. It's the sort of thing you can hear in other bars, if you' re lucky.

But at Hamilton's the talk always returns to Saipan, its characters and deals, its endless redefinition of itself: an island cuffed around by history, occupied by genocidal Spaniards, by firm but fair Germans, by hardworking Japanese colonists, by Americans who didn't know what to do with the place but didn't let it go until, at last, the Saipanese decided they didn't want to let go of America. There's a kind of hurly-burly free masonry of Saipan, among the drinkers who've stayed for years and people like me, a recidivist visitor. And, late at night, this brings me to a question I put to two long-time residents. "You two," I begin, "came here when I did — what, thirty years ago? — and fell in love with the place. And stayed. I didn't stay. But l keep coming back. So the question is, if we came here now, came as the young men we used to be, would we fall in love with Saipan again? Today's Saipan?"

There's a pause, not a long one, but enough for me to wish that Wilbur Hamilton could answer, too. His vote might carry the day. Fair enough. It's his place. His picture's on the wall, along with John Wayne's, his sayings printed on T-shirts, his widow sitting in a kitchen that turns out the same meal I relished thirty years ago: sashimi appetizer, followed by chicken-fried steaks, washed down with beer and tequila shooters — the perfect meal. But the answer from the rest of us, when it comes, is No: we would not fall in love again here. And what came to me before returns with renewed force. Saipan isn't an island anymore. Forget island images from literature, film, television: islands of *Gilligan, Treasure, Fantasy, Shipwreck, Devil's, Swiss Family Robinson, Shakespeare's Tempest, Doctors Moreau* and *No.* They're irrelevant. Forget supposed island styles, languorous, easy-going, long memories and short working days, a small world where everyone knows or sort of knows everyone else. Forget the conventional island adjectives: remote, self-sufficient, isolated, insular. On Saipan, they no longer apply.

"A Grateful Island Remembers" is the theme of the sixtieth-anniversary celebration, and on the Monday after my arrival back on Saipan the "History Alive" seminars begin. Part of me has been dreading this. It's been fun roaming the island, surprising old friends; I have more of them than I realized. And island reunions are peculiar. Since you've already come and gone, there's an assumption that, the odds are, you won't be back; the world's full of other places, bigger and more important places by all conventional measures. So when you come across people here, or they come across you, there's surprise, even shock, something approaching time warp. We meet and it's easy to talk about old times on an island so drastically transformed. Lots of things are better than they used to be — housing, shopping, eating, medical care. And I have to be careful, careful, because I knew them when they were underdogs and now they are overlords, and Americans as well. Step carefully, I tell myself, avoid sounding like too many visitors, mourning the loss of simpler, poorer times. That's the worst kind of condescension: you're living in paradise, take it from me, don't change a thing, small is beautiful and the simple life is best. Still, there's no escaping a sense of loss and puzzlement. People are better off than ever, better than their old partners in the Trust Territory and much better than most Pacific Islands which, once you get past the beaches and the palm trees, are poor and troubled places. But the people I meet are worried about the money that's come in from outside, the waves of workers, worried about prosperity and vulnerability. So we talk about an island that's gone, a time that's past: it's what we have in common. And now, as the "History Alive" seminars kick off, I'm plunged into the past, part of an ultimate reunion — Americans who came in across the reef, under fire, returning to the island they liberated.

"Liberated," as it turns out, might not be the right word. That is one of the first messages to arrive, as proceedings begin in the Hyatt's Sand Castle Room, a lounge-showroom that usually hosts a Las Vegas-type show, Siegfried-and-Royish, with tigers and chorus girls. Sitting at dining tables or on soft, curving banquettes are about eighty people, some local, some visitors. The first thing we hear, from Dirk Ballendorf, a former Peace Corps director, now a professor at the University of Guam, is about the nature of pre-war Saipan, and about the liberation that wasn't quite as advertised. The Japanese ousted the Germans in 1914, he points out, and had been on Saipan for thirty years. They didn't occupy a hostile country, they inherited a colony. The Saipanese were dominated, marginalized, but not enslaved. Outnumbered by Japanese, Okinawan, and Korean settlers brought in to fish, farm, and run the sugar industry, they were a generation or two from being absorbed into the Japanese empire. The war interrupted one process of assimilation and began another.

If it wasn't quite a liberation, it was a battle, a slaughter. That becomes clear in the afternoon, when we get a reading of two Japanese journals that were found in the battlefield. It's haunting stuff, if you care about the ones on the other side. A civilian describes his first sight of 500 ships offshore: "vessels, vessels and more vessels. Hundreds of military ships and the shadows in the setting sun covered the waters of Tanapag." A medic witnesses suicides and requested beheadings at the end of the battle and goes to his death regretting "that I have nothing to report when my life is fluttering away like a flower petal to become part of… the soil."

A "Veterans Campfire" is scheduled for the evening after the first day of seminars. I don't want to go. The Battle for Saipan has enveloped me for several days and I am starting to chafe. There have been parades, interviews, speeches, a U.S.O. show, a Catholic mass, battlefield tours, and fireworks, and this thing tonight has the whiff of summer camp about it. Besides, when I arrive it's raining, but not quite hard enough for me to escape. I see two tents, one with a bunch of veterans sitting on bleachers, the other with spectators in folding chairs. Between, there's a campfire that, I guess, is supposed to invite storytelling. I've got my doubts. In a minute, I'm off to Hamilton's. But then, to my surprise, something interesting begins. People begin to talk, people who've been carrying things inside them for years, just waiting for a chance to testify on Saipan, in front of an audience of strangers. Sure, it starts slowly, with accounts of saki, a pet monkey, a chance meeting with a hometown buddy: stuff out of Beetle Bailey and Sergeant Bilko. But then, it changes. He's not clear whether it happened on Saipan or Tarawa, but one man recalls a wall, it doesn't matter where, a wall with Americans on one side and Japanese on the other. An officer invites him to go first over the wall. He declines, says he'd be happy to be led into the battle. It sounds good-humored, the kind of banter you'd hear in a movie. The officer goes over the wall, a second officer follows, then a private. The speaker's turn comes. On the other side, his three predecessors lie dead. And, hearing this, I know I'll be late to Hamilton's. A Marine wounded on Saipan recalls waking up on a hospital ship. There were nurses and ice cream. And he was crying about being out of the battle, the beginning of a guilt he would carry, he says, for the rest of his life. Now, a woman arises from the other side of the campfire, my side, where spectators and locals sit. It turns out to be a Saipanese woman who offers a harrowing account of moving between lines, under fire, most of her ten-member family dying one by one, and the speaker fearing "that we would be buried by a tank that ran over us and no one would know where we died." Another woman, one year old during the battle, recalls what she was told: that an American named Rafael brought her milk. She's been searching records for years, trying to locate her Rafael. Now it's an American woman's time; she's been sitting among the veterans, and when she speaks her voice is on the edge of breaking. She pauses here and there to pull herself together. Her husband, recently dead, was Robert North, a Stanford political scientist, a specialist in the quantitative analysis of war, when it breaks out, seemingly inevitable, when it is avoided. "He thought of Saipan as the defining moment of his life," his wife says. "Bob always told me that after the Battle of Saipan, every day was a bonus for him, every day..." But the campfire belongs, I think, to an ex-Marine from Philadelphia, a dapper, well-adjusted fellow, the last man

I'd expect to speak here. Well, he stipulates, he's not the sort of man who is haunted by war, the way some veterans are. He doesn't awaken at night, sweating and screaming. But he can still see those people jumping off Suicide Cliff. "I remember the way they floated down... with no movement... not even the movement that a falling feather makes. They just drifted through the air. Children and parents. That's not a nightmare. It's a horrible memory, though —"

Memory. It's been dogging me, along with its close companions, time and age. I drive this island and at every tum memory stands there, like a hitchhiker. On a new island, among new businesses, new deals, new fortunes, I shuttle back and forth between places and people I remember, that remember me. And if it's that way for me, what about the veterans? They're a tiny majority on the island, ghosts-in-the-making. Granted, this is their week, and their hosts have done everything that might be expected, down to the commemorative medals that'll be awarded tonight. But look in the hotel lobbies and it's golfers and shoppers from Japan and, increasingly, China who come to Saipan now. We — I and the veterans and the Saipanese who care enough to come to the seminars — are Saipan then. But today, in our carpeted, upholstered, air-conditioned campground, I hear a story that gives me goosebumps.

"I am delighted, deliriously delighted," the speaker begins, "to be here today. I am delighted to be anywhere, sixty years later." The crowd laughs appreciatively. What the casualties of war amounted to is nothing, compared to the toll of dead, wounded, and missing in action in recent years. The speaker is retired Lieutenant General Lawrence Snowden, a Marine officer on Saipan. He's sharply dressed, well organized, no-nonsense. I talked to him briefly on Tinian, when he explained what flame-throwers did to men in bunkers: bum or suffocate. Now he delivers a brisk, crisp account of the Battle of Saipan. "The soldier's view of war," he grants, "is narrow and shallow." Snowden gives a larger perspective on a brutal battle that went well, a coordinated application of naval gunfire, aerial bombing, and overwhelming forces hitting the invasion beaches. As he tells it, there was no question of who would win, only at what cost. The goosebumps come at the end. He's been asked to discuss personal experiences, Snowden says, and this is something soldiers avoid. "They don't think that non-veterans have the background to understand." Still, he tries to oblige. He talks of advancing through sugar cane fields, green and dense or black and sooty. He recalls swarms of flies, "green and black, ugly and vicious" that hitched a ride on a forkful of food as it went into Marines' mouths. There's another round of sympathetic laughter and I sense that Snowden could stop now; perhaps he wonders if he should, if he's said enough. But he proceeds and the result is unforgettable.

"We were moving through the edges of Chalan Kanoa," he says, "and we came into a clearing and there were fifteen or twenty people I took to be native islanders, Chamorros — and all of them were dead. Except for a baby, a year old maybe, crying, clinging to its mother's arm." Snowden lifted the baby into his arms, summoned a Chamorro speaker from behind the lines. And just then telling the part of the story, Snowden breaks up,

ambushed by emotions back then, ambushed now. The nature of war overwhelmed him; he says he thought of his own son, back home, whom he might never see again. He wept. He weeps. "A baby in my arms," he says. "I held her tight. It all welled up." He stops and collects himself. "This woman… I don't know… she'd be sixty or sixty-one years old now," Snowden resumes. "And I'd love to hold her in my arms again." Another pause. "That was the sort of emotional experience I'm not supposed to have had," he concludes. "But I did."
Nearly ninety, nearly deaf, Enola Gay pilot Paul Tibbetts is Saipan's star attraction. Under bruise-colored skies, hundreds of people converge on the American Memorial Park, sitting patiently through introductory oratory from ten different agencies. I can't count the number of times a politician or military representative tells us that "freedom isn't free." Nature itself protests: just as Commonwealth Governor Juan Babauta stands up to speak, the skies open up with one of those sudden storms that occur only in the tropics. It rains, hard, harder, hardest, and just when you think things are at the worst, the rain storm ratchets up another notch. People at the edge of the tent move further inside but then sudden cascades come off the sagging tent and I am sitting and sharing an umbrella with an old friend, giggling like a kid. But when the storm eases, Paul Tibbetts's time comes. I interviewed Tibbetts years ago, when a television movie was made about his mission to Hiroshima. I knew that he was a polite, measured, considerate man who went out of his way to disappoint some people's expectations. No, he did not hate Japanese, he did not love war, and he suffered no doubt, guilt, or regret about the role that history assigned him. He didn't agonize then

and he doesn't now. A standing ovation greets him, a white-haired gent in a blue shirt. Camera flashes light up the podium, coming from all directions. Folksy and good-humored, Tibbetts teases the politicians and brass who preceded him, "reciting their pedigrees." And then, as I later learn, he discards his prepared text and embarks on a speech that begins with his service in Europe. It's quirky, detailed, rambling, and slow. After nearly half an hour, he is still stateside, in the early stages of preparing the A-bomb mission. By my estimate, he is another twenty minutes away from Tinian, fifteen more from Hiroshima. And I suspect his intention is never to get there, never to deliver the sort of heartfelt soliloquy the audience awaits. At last — and it' s a mercy — I see someone approach from the sidelines and slip a note into Tibbetts' s hand. "I've got five minutes left," Tibbetts announces. And, though some in the audience would listen to him for another hour, Tibbetts complies. "We got the job done," he concludes, "and that's all there is to say."

How to treat this island, that compels and appalls? Battlefield island, Commonwealth island, on the edge of American power, on the edge of the Pacific, straddling spheres of influence, dodgy and opportunistic. I'm the last speaker, I close the show. Do I mention that the Commonwealth agreement was a deal worked out between Saipan' s Washington lawyers and Washington's Washington lawyers? That it amounted to American citizenship, home delivered, halfway around the world? How will the vets feel if I tell them that no matter what they gave of themselves on Saipan, they cannot buy land here? Saipanese retiring on generous government pensions purchase homes in the United States, but the veterans, gratefully remembered as they are, remain outsiders. Do I mention that? Do I include this? Maybe not. Meanwhile I listen to an old Saipanese friend, an insurance man, Dave Sablan, begin the last day's seminar. Sablan's done well over the years. Cocky and self-assured, he introduces a pair of pretty Filipina employees who'll make sure his slides pop up on screen on cue. Saipan was "infested" with Japanese just before the invasion he says: the garrison was swollen with crews off sunken supply ships, often unarmed. Sablan and his family hid in a cave near Mount Tagpochau. They'd been told that the Americans were monsters, tall, cruel, lethal. When they eventually were enticed out of their hiding place, their first Marine was four feet eight inches tall, skinny, red-haired, maybe 120 pounds. And he was wearing a crucifix. Suddenly, Sablan loses it, covering his face with his hands, swiping at tears. "That's when they had us," he said; "when we saw the crucifix." He's followed by Teddy Draper, a Navajo code talker who recalls running through an alley of blasted bodies in Iwo Jima. Then, for the last time, we break for lunch. Then, around two, just as the crowd is nodding off into a post-prandial siesta, my time will come. But there's something powerful about being last. When I'm done, we all leave this room that I've gotten used to and go out into daylight and heat, a hotel lobby full of luggage and golf bags and people who don't care about what brought us here. We leave and go in separate directions, never to reconvene. And we leave soon: my flight is tomorrow, at 4:30 in the morning. I wish it were not so soon. I could talk myself into staying a while.

It's easy to be scathing about Saipan. There's a website operated by someone anonymous called saipansucks.com, a catch-basin of expatriate complaints. Recently it's been running a contest for an island slogan. The idea is you take "Welcome to Saipan" and add a phrase. Submissions so far include Welcome to Saipan: the Mexico of the Pacific; You Get What You Pay For; We Avenge World War 11 One Japanese Tourist at a Time; America's Biggest Welfare Client; The Other West Virginia; Where Every Non-Local Is a Doormat; Where America Ends. These disappointments don't come out of nowhere, but my feelings about Saipan are mixed and tangled. So is my speech. I will go out, get them to laugh and cry, knock a little, boost a little, celebrate and damn. And remember. That's the most important thing. To remember and to be remembered. The veterans know that and more: that when people die, they die; when they're forgotten, they die forever. And this island, with its self-sacrificing and self-dealing, is a place that resonates memory. More important than anything else I say today, every mixed review, close call, up or down, is memory. Some of that's in my speech, near the end. "In a forgetting time, attention span shortening, reaction time lengthening, memory is the most important thing, morally imperative. People need to remember as they grow old; so do nations." Having memories, making memories, on an island with a history. I'll take this place over all the sandy beaches, the palmy atolls, the carefree islands in the world. Saying some hard things but nothing so hard that it would foreclose my coming back here.

And I'll close with something from Siegfried Sassoon, a poem set in the trenches of World War I, not the beachheads of World War II. But it will serve the veterans as well. And me, until my next trip.

Have you forgotten yet? ...
Look down, and swear by the slain of the War that you'll never forget.
Do you remember that hour of din before the attack —
And the anger, the blind compassion that seized and shocked you then
As you peered at the doomed and haggard faces of your men?
Do you remember the stretcher-cases lurching back
With dying eyes and lolling heads, those ashen-grey
Masks of the lads who once were keen and kind and gay?
Have you forgotten yet? ...
Look up, and swear by the green of the Spring that you'll never forget.

Saipan: From Then to Now

The Contemporary Pacific, Volume 18, No. 1, 2006

When I left the island of Saipan after two years of Peace Corps service in the late 1960s, I promised myself that I would return as often as possible. That's not the same as living there, certainly not the same as having been born there. But it's a promise that I have kept and still keep. I was back in the early 1970s to work for the Congress of Micronesia's Future Political Status Commission, in the mid-1970s to work for the Micronesian Constitutional Convention. Magazine assignments brought.me back, as did the research for my 1991 book *The Edge of Paradise: America in Micronesia.* Most recently, I was invited back to give a speech in connection with the sixtieth anniversary of the World War II battle for Saipan. What follows is an edited version of "Saipan: From Then to Now," delivered to an audience of veterans and Saipan residents on 16 June 2004.

I'll begin with a scrap, just a scrap, of poetry. If you travel around Australia and drop in for an early evening drink at a Returned Servicemen's Club, you'll find that, at precisely 7 PM, the lights will flicker, the place will fall silent, the drinking will stop, and someone will read this 1914 poem by Laurence Binyon, a poem in memory of young men who died.

They shall not grow old, as we that are left grow old:
Age shall not weary them, nor the years condemn.
At the going down of the sun and in the morning
We will remember them…

Laurence Binyon, *For the Fallen*

Now, this is a time of remembering on Saipan. I have reflected about what I might say to you or whether I had any right to stand before you at all. I was not a part of the battle, and whatever my times on Saipan over the years have amounted to, they were never a matter of life and death. So what business does a former Peace Corps volunteer have at a battle memorial? And what can someone from a small college in Ohio have to say about Saipan, where he doesn't live, doesn't own property, doesn't vote?

The answer is that I keep thinking about Saipan, wherever I am, and keep returning; and each return — this one no exception — is more surprising than the last. Saipan is an island that is defined by its ability to reinvent itself, to startle, intimidate, charm, and appall. It's a place that can — over and over again — win your heart, and break it, and take it back.

I wonder what it looks like — make that, feels like — to those of you who saw this place in 1944. It must be as if you have traveled through two dimensions: not just space — many long miles — but time as well, sixty years of it. Half a world, more than half a century: that's quite a trip. It speaks well of you that you have come, and of the Northern Marianas government that it has welcomed you. There will always be a place for you here, I suspect. I remember a line of William Faulkner's: "The past isn't over," he said. "It isn't even past."

This afternoon, I'll attempt to connect the then — the battleground Saipan of history books and newsreels — with the now, the rich and bewildering island you encounter today. Let me start with this: As we mark the sixtieth anniversary of the battle of Saipan, it must be pointed out that World War II was not fought to liberate Saipan. The fate of this island — a legal League of Nations mandate under Japanese administration, an island well on the way to being absorbed within the Japanese imperium — was on no one's list of primary, secondary, or incidental war goals. In war, as in real estate, location is everything, and Saipan's location on the route to Japan is what mattered. Still, it is equally true that, whether by accident or design, the battle of Saipan was the beginning of an otherwise improbable engagement between a post-World War II superpower — never more powerful than then — and a small Pacific island.

From the start it was a complicated relationship, involving affection and force, bona fide goodwill and cold-eyed calculation from both sides. It was not entirely military, not even in the early years, and is not entirely civilian, not even now. After the war, the people in the US State Department, not to mention those at the United Nations, stipulated that the captured Micronesian islands should be developed economically and politically. Our UN trusteeship specified that self-government or independence (or both) would eventually be offered. What's more, it was understood that the trusteeship would be kept intact, as a whole: no changing borders, no division, no side deals. But the people at the defense department had their own requirements: understandably they wanted access to the islands they had captured at such cost. They had plans for parts of Micronesia: the Marshalls, Palau, the Northern Marianas, especially Saipan and Tinian. And they insisted on the right of denial for all of Micronesia: no other nation could establish a competing presence here, military or commercial. Furthermore, though all the islands were a UN trusteeship, this particular trusteeship was a strategic one, not at the mercy of hurly-burly, free-swinging orators in the UN General Assembly. Instead, Micronesia was subject to the controlling veto of the United States in the UN Security Council.

What it all comes to is that tensions existed in the US approach to Micronesia from the beginning — contradictions and cross-purposes, especially between the departments of state and defense, and especially concerning Saipan. The US Naval Administration ended in 1952, when the US Department of Interior took over the Trust Territory. But soon, the Northern Marianas were given back to the military, mainly because a secret guerilla-training operation was based on Saipan. The Naval Technical Training Unit (NTTU, it was called), an educational institution whose graduates — Nationalist Chinese and possibly Indonesian — have no alumni association and no class reunions. The locals called it "the secret place." They talked of late-night flights coming into Kagman Field, of passengers shunted onto buses with blacked-out windows. Years later, I heard of people who lived on Saipan in the sixties meeting other people who acknowledged that they, too, had spent time on Saipan. When? they would be asked. In the fifties, they would reply, and a curtain would come down on the conversation. A vow of secrecy. Who couldn't be curious about the Naval Technical Training Unit? I checked aerial photographs, looking for NTTU installations. The most promising areas were whited-out. I hiked the boondocks they once used: a foundation with a rusted-out Coke machine was all I found. Even with a huge cash advance from a publisher, subpoena powers, a battery of lawyers, and many syringes of sodium pentothal, a writer might not capture the Naval Technical Training Unit — a great story that, almost certainly, will never be told. Not until this shadowy outfit decamped was Saipan placed under Trust Territory, that is, US Department of Interior control. That was in the early sixties. A few years later I arrived; I am glad that my time to discover Saipan was then, not later, not now. I'm not sure I could hack it now or would want to try, or that I would fall for the place as I did back then.

In launching a large Micronesia program, the Peace Corps had advertised, only half ironically, that it was going to paradise. The result was an ambitious, overextended, and controversial program involving hundreds of volunteers. We joked that if the same ratio of volunteers to locals prevailed in, say, India, there would be no young people left in the United States.

The Saipan we came to was no paradise, that was clear. Almost a quarter century had passed since the shooting had stopped, and yet the place was still shaped, defined, by the battle that had been fought here. Long after the combat stopped, long after the naval administration walked away from its camps and Quonsets and airfields, the island was... well... haunted. It was like a theater that had been abandoned by actors and by audience, a place still littered with costumes and props, ticket stubs and programs in the aisles. Have you ever, driving around America, gone past an old outdoor drive-in theater, the big screen still standing, weeds in the parking lot, long semicircular rows of those little parking-meter-like poles evenly spaced, and the ruins of a rickety, graffiti-marked projection booth in the middle of it all? That was what Saipan felt like.

It had a kind of sullen magic. Scarred, handsome, and in its way, beautiful. It invited exploring. It made you think. And it was all about the past; it was about some of you who gather here now. It was about you, this sighting out from the invasion beach at landing craft and tanks impaled on the reef. It was about you, when I went swimming off the rusting breakwaters and half-sunken barges at Charley Dock. It was about you, traveling in and off the islands, waiting at little Kobler Field for a DC-3. You were there, your spirit lingered at Isley Field, with overgrown bunkers and revetments, all the giant footsteps of another time. Saipan then was one of those rare, dear places where you could confront history without a ticket, a tape-recorded spiel, a forced march through a museum, and a sign warning you about all the things you weren't supposed to do. In the villages — Garapan, Susupe, Chalan Kanoa — it was about you, in the remnants and ruins of destroyed Japanese buildings, bullet-pocked walls and cisterns, overgrown gardens; about you as well in the scrap metal and lumber taken from the emptied internment camps, hammered into houses, and collected and re-hammered after typhoons, when people came back from bunkers and old Japanese buildings where they had taken shelter during the storms. You were on the roads, in surplus jeeps the Saipanese had purchased at $1 each. You were in the roads themselves, those roads that, more than anything else, made Saipan special: it was the only Trust Territory island west of Majuro where you could spend more than a minute in third gear. And what places there were to go to! There was Capitol Hill, up on Mount Tagpochau; the locals called it Mount Olympus. You couldn't see it from out at sea, couldn't see it from down below at sea level, and you couldn't see it if you were a member of a UN visiting mission.

By 1967 the former NTTU headquarters had become the seat of the Trust Territory government, with the high commissioner in the highest house, and other worthies, including a handful of Micronesians, down below, all of them in a little America of airy, spacious typhoon-proof houses surrounded by grassy, well-barbered lawns, with a view far, far out to sea; in the mornings, you could see clear to Anatahan Island, if you knew just where to look. Sure, I was a Peace Corps Volunteer, I lived way down below, in a funky house with holes in the roof and floor, but could I be blamed if, then and for years to come, I defined success in life — having it made — as a house on Capitol Hill? That, too, was a legacy of the war. The past was all around: the Sugar King Monument, the jail where Amelia Earhart was said to have languished and died. Off the road — sometimes, just off the road — were tanks, bunkers, and debris you'd drive past every day, never suspecting they were there, until a typhoon peeled back the brush and exposed the marks of war. But no place so rewarded exploring as the Marpi District at the north end, toward Suicide and Banzai cliffs. Most of the place was off limits then: this was where the ammunition for the planned invasion of Japan had been stored. After Colonel Paul Tibbets intervened, the ordnance was a headache. Shipping it off island was expensive and pointless; dumping it into the sea was laborious and dangerous. What to do? Someone evidently suggested destroying the stuff by detonating it in place. It half worked: the shells were scattered, higgledy-piggledy, all over the place — in the open, buried in the ground, half in, half out — and often still intact. This led to a local industry, a kind of reckless handicraft: people slipping into Marpi to strip valuable copper and bronze fittings off the still-lethal ammunition. The clinking of hammers against metal sounded through the boondock nights, sometimes punctuated by the blast of an exploding shell. By the time I arrived, a wry and memorable fellow named Steve Aiken led a crew, disarming and collecting the bombs. I used a version of him in my first novel; later he attempted a novel himself. Aiken picked his way through flatlands, past the so-called Last Command Post, the caves that had been blasted shut in battle, that now, with time, were slowly opening, revealing sake bottles, mess kits, helmets, bones. It could make a person thoughtful. My guide to the cliffs, from which enemy soldiers and civilians jumped to the death in what may have been the worst mass suicide in history, was Tony Benavente, a policeman when I met him, who had been present when the American invaders tried to coax frightened people into surrendering. I remember the way he pointed at the cliffs, the height, the jump, the dying fall. And I remember wondering aloud which would have been worse, going off Suicide Cliff onto hard ground hundreds of feet below, or going off Banzai Cliff into turbulent, beautifully blue, shark-infested waves. I remember Tony Benavente's shrug.

The battles we remember this week were resonant and pervasive. It wasn't just a matter of marks on the land; it was reflected also in island life, not only in roads and jeeps and houses, not just in the remnants and — to put it directly — remains of a great battle; it was right there on island tables, in the enduring love of Spam, in the leftover knives, forks, and plates you saw at island parties, with navy insignia and initials. It was in the songs that sounded out of jukeboxes in ramshackle bars along Beach Road. The bars were never busier than on those tumultuous, loose-lipped Payday Fridays, every other week, when government employees invested their pay in endless Budweisers. In the background, the music was American country western — plangent, plaintive left-behind tunes like "Please Release Me, Let Me Go"— which summarizes the Saipanese attitude towards the trusteeship and thus qualifies as an informal anthem of today's commonwealth. Or "Am I So Easy to Forget?" and — I kid you not — "You Are My Sunshine." And there were certain phrases you could hear that reflected military history. A new hire was always "coming on board." And if you returned here after years away, some old friend would ask, "Where are you stationed now?" It was more than l could manage to reply that, well, I wasn't really "stationed" anywhere. But the largest legacy of the battle of Saipan was in the Saipanese regard for the United States. On other Micronesian islands, the war had swept quickly by, as at Kwajalein and Enewetok, or been confined to specific secondary islands, like Peleliu and Angaur in Palau. Other places — Truk, Yap, Ponape, Kusaie — had been spared land fighting. Here in the Northern Marianas the battle had been followed by camps, roads, bases, new construction, secret training operations. The military left a larger, longer mark. No wonder that, when I arrived in 1967, it was easy to see that the Saipanese weren't happy with being part of, indeed the capital of, the Trust Territory of Pacific Islands, the scattered and improbable "TT."

In many ways, the TT was mission impossible. As editor of a magazine called *The Micronesian Reporter* and author/editor of an island guidebook, I learned to rattle off the following sentences from memory: "The Trust Territory has 2,141 islands with an aggregate landmass half the size of Rhode Island scattered over an area the size of the continental United States, and a population of 120,000 that could be-possibly should be accommodated in the Pasadena Rose Bowl. It has six districts, nine mutually-unintelligible languages, and a subsistence economy of fishing and farming, as well as the copra trade, scrap metal, and government employment… "About then, people's eyes started glazing over, like yours. If I persisted, it would be to add that this was the last post-World War II UN Trusteeship, and that America, which (perish the thought) was not a colonial power, was supposed to offer the people a choice about their future government and political status — eventually, sort of, somehow, maybe…

The Saipanese disliked the Trust Territory and in a moment I will tell you why. Before that, I want to do something that I never thought I'd do. Way too late for it to make a difference to anyone but me, I would like to say a few good words about the TT government. They got a lot of bad press from a lot of people, myself included. The "Rust Territory" it was called: second-rate war-surplus equipment, second-rate war-surplus officials, time servers, political hacks, career paper pushers, friends of well-placed friends, all hunkering down or hiding out in a comfy cul-de-sac. What we had here was a holding operation, low in budget, low in vision, energy, purpose. And there was something to this criticism. There were some remarkable people — I was tempted to say cases — out here, people who just weren't up to much. And, caught as it was between cross-purposes, keeping the islands secure for the military while somehow advancing self-determination, between developing the place and yet preserving it, the Trust Territory had not accomplished a great deal. Should they keep alive the world of thatched roofs, traditional navigation, subsistence fishing and agriculture? Or import California, the sooner the better? The Japanese had been busy in Micronesia, busy with plantations — sugar cane especially, coffee, even rice. There was fishing, there was mining. There was colonization: streets, trains, buildings, temples, gardens. Settlers and settlements. Though the Trust Territory made progress in health care, education, local government, they hadn't revived the private sector — and the memory, the very ruins of Japanese enterprise, were a source of constant reproach, reflected in the bitter, much-quoted epithet that the Spanish came for god, the Germans came for gold, the Japanese came for glory, and the Americans came for good.

Still, looking back on that admittedly torpid time, I remember people who loved this place, who worked quietly and cared. Whatever they attempted — their wins and losses — they were determined that no harm should be done. That's not a recipe for robust growth, granted, but I would pause before condemning what can come off as a condescending, go-slow, the-islands-are-fragile, the-people-aren't-ready attitude. People thought it was patronizing. Maybe so. It was, after all, a trusteeship. But when I return here, I find myself asking whether the pell-mell exploitation, the get-rich deals that occurred in a few years of self-government don't far outweigh what happened during the long yawning decades of trusteeship. And though the Trust Territory reposes in history's dustbin, it must be granted that there was an idealism underlying the notion of a nation of federated, disparate states. Pathetic as it was, the Trust Territory, if it had worked — a huge if — might have had something to teach Kashmir, Iraq, the former Yugoslavia, the Sudan. But, as it happened, other lessons were coming.

The Saipanese, for years, petitioned for separation. They petitioned visiting UN missions, they petitioned at the UN, they passed resolution after resolution, they invited other nations, numerous other nations, to put in a bid, make a play, anything but this captivity, this long sleepwalk. Whether in reunion with Guam or on their own, the Northern Marianas wanted out of Micronesia and into a close permanent relationship with the United States. And — here's where the past impinges — the reason or part of the reason for this was the lesson in US power and largesse first demonstrated on the invasion beach, in the battle we remember now. Everything follows from that, every intended or unintended result, every consequence and every accident.

Well, there is something to be said for knowing what you want and working for it steadfastly, through years of rejection. Sooner or later you win, and you only need to win once. In the late sixties, the Trust Territory's Congress of Micronesia began serious negotiations with the United States about the future. The other five districts wanted a loose relationship with the United States. They knew they needed aid and protection, but they insisted on sovereignty, on control of their lands, on the option — later on — to change or end their arrangement with the United States. Simply put, they wanted the advantages of dependence and the benefits of independence. Free association, they called it. So they rejected the idea of annexation to Hawai'i and thus to the United States, they rejected the chance to become a US territory, and another offer, to become a Commonwealth. This was too much for Saipan to bear, and in Palau, in April 1972 — I was in the room — the other Micronesians at last acceded to the Marianas' request for separate talks with the United States, an offer the United

States instantly accepted. With that, the chance of the Trust Territory producing a united Micronesia died; this not-quite colony, this accidental state, with its six-star flag and a national anthem based on a melody of Brahms, perished. And the US Commonwealth that welcomes you today was born. I wonder what you make of it. I wonder what I make of it. I was here, in 1975, when 78.8 percent of Northern Marianas voters decided to become US citizens and to make their islands a permanent part of the United States. It was an emotional moment and the emotions, in my case, were mixed. It was touching, it was a tribute, to see Saipan and the other Northern Marianas freely elect to join the United States, to see years of determination at last rewarded. It wasn't what the war was about, nor was it the aim of the naval administration of the islands. It wasn't what the US Departments of Interior and State had planned and, for sure, it wasn't what the United Nations had envisioned. But doesn't that make it all the more impressive? Think of it, coming back here, greeting old friends as fellow countrymen, fellow citizens. How can I, you — anybody — fail to approve? And, speaking of happy endings, shouldn't it be pointed out that America's three predecessors — Spain, Germany, Japan — never dreamed of offering or honoring the kind of choice the Marianas made?

But... well, there's always a but... my emotions were mixed. And are. Put aside as so much youthful fantasy the idea of a united Micronesia coming out of the Trust Territory. Enough of that. Put aside anybody's pleasure in seeing friends get what they want: better houses, higher land values, cars, traffic lights, duty-free shops, a Washington office. Put aside that the Northern Marianas' escape from the other Micronesian states had its pragmatic side: the escape of the rich, or potentially rich, from the relatively — in some cases, irretrievably — poor. Let's be frank — there were two measures of island wealth at that time. One was real or imagined military value to the United States. In short: location, location, location. This, the Northern Marianas had. The other was imminent potential for tourism: access for warm-weathering visitors from Japan. The Northern Marianas had that as well. So what we saw was a separation of the haves from the have-nots. And, lest anyone suggest that the Northern Marianas were particularly uncharitable to less well-endowed neighbors, let's note that the division of erstwhile Trust Territory along economic — and racial — lines continued. The Marshalls and Palau, both with military assets, peeled off from Truk, Ponape, Yap, and the new state of Kosrae. Everybody was taking their best shot, making their best deal. And the people of the Northern Marianas joined the long list of those who came to the United States for reasons of opportunity, economic opportunity. Nothing new about that, nothing wrong. These seekers after a better life surely outnumber the persecuted pilgrims, hounded idealists, political refugees. They include my parents, and possibly yours.

And that is the end of all my putting aside and the beginning of my perplexity. Anyone who was on an island that was converted, overnight, into American soil, its people, overnight, into American citizens, had to wonder. Those parents of mine traveled from Europe — Germany — to the United States. They renounced one nationality, one loyalty, for another. They took a voyage, made a pledge, learned a new language. They came to America. But America came to Saipan: citizenship was conferred, on terms that Saipan's Washington lawyers and Washington's Washington lawyers worked out. I couldn't help wondering what America, and American citizenship, would mean under these circumstances. American citizenship, home-delivered. Was it about shared values? Or shared value? I'm still wondering, still watching. It's what keeps me coming back. What does it mean to become American in this way, at this date, at this distance?

Now, in an island vastly transformed since becoming part of America, there remains cause for celebration and concern. What I love, maybe more now than before, is the wild-card vitality, the buzz and hurly-burly, the characters who land — in some cases, wash up — here: searchers, dreamers, tax-dodgers, flimflam men... the hits just keep coming. What characters, what schemes, especially in the early years: an x-rated Doonesbury cartoon. This was let's-make-a-deal time, the coming of disco, duty-free karaoke, poker machines, etc., etc. A time in which opportunity shaded into opportunism. The world discovered Saipan; Saipan discovered the world. Things got complicated and still are. The Saipan tourist industry is at the mercy of ups and downs in Japan, the wanderlust of mainland Chinese, the health of airlines, the outbreak of SARS (Severe Acute Respiratory Syndrome), the risk of terrorism. The garment industry thrives in the shadow of regulations, soon to go into effect, that will permit Chinese garments made in China into the US market. Will Chinese need to come to Saipan to sew? In its moment of greatest strength, Saipan is singularly vulnerable to outside forces beyond its control. All this is another way of saying it has ceased in an important way to be an island at all. Forget your images of island life: Robinson Crusoe, Treasure Island, Shakespeare's Tempest, Fantasy Island, Napoleon on St. Helena. Forget the familiar island adjectives: remote, isolated, lonely, insular, self-sufficient. They don't apply. Saipan's not an island anymore. It's all connected.

The island's main export may be irony. I saw the first Japanese tourists in the late sixties: decorous, dark-suited, camera-toting groups, middle-aged and older. I attended the opening of the first hotel, the Royal Taga. First and last, I thought. Was I wrong! Who could have guessed that a World War II battleground would turn into a Japanese Florida? Or that its transformation would mimic the 1944 campaign, first taking the invasion beaches, then heading north toward Marpi, with duty-free shopping, souvenir and convenience stores, gaming emporia, and shooting galleries following along behind? And, among these nearly 500,000 visitors per year, there are fewer and fewer who come for the reasons that unite us today. They walk past pillboxes and monuments on their way to the beach. Was there a battle here? Well, that was then and this is now. A famous victory? Never mind: sunburn lotion is their armor. Against this tide of indifference and forgetting, the memories we share and renew may amount to more than history. They may offer guidance in times ahead.

Talk about garment industries, talk about hotels, and realize that they have one thing in common: a reliance on outside capital and outside labor. The Saipanese are agents, middlemen — not bosses, and rarely employees. Where are the Saipanese? The most enthusiastic celebrants of the US Commonwealth — and there is much to celebrate: hospitals, businesses, a likable junior college — turn quiet when I inquire. The Saipanese are outnumbered, nearly two-to-one, on their own island, that's for sure. Outnumbered by those waves of foreign workers, garment makers, security guards, barbers and beauticians, hostesses and maids, farmers and hardhats who have come to do the island's heavy lifting. There were around 11,000 people in the Northern Marianas in 1967, mostly local, and now there are 75,000, mostly alien. Be careful what you wish for. Saipanese are a minority on their own islands — an elite minority, to be sure, and determined to stay that way, but a minority nonetheless. What, then, are they up to? What is their work, job, occupation, trade, calling? Their purpose or their passion? This is something that they may still be discovering. It's taking time. For the moment, most island citizens who work are employed by local and commonwealth government. That is cause for wonder. It will take a few trips to know whether the situation I've described can last: an entrenched government contending with outside money, transient workers. I will not predict the worst: the island has a way of dodging bullets, pulling through. It has some magic. But if I predicted happy endings, we'd have to define terms. That's another trip.

I'll say this: there will be more battles on Saipan — not like the one you fought, but battles nonetheless, with the character and direction of the island at stake. For now, tragedy and accident, coincidence and fortune have played a part in this island and its history: people acting selflessly, selfishly, the same people sometimes, motives mixed and tangled. This is the history that connects then and now. And, as ever, location. The northward flight of bomb-carrying B-29s back then, the southward flight of tourist-packed 747s, today and tomorrow.

Thank you for coming and remembering. In a forgetting time, attention spans shortening, reaction times lengthening, it's the most important thing, morally imperative. People need to remember as they grow old; so do islands; so do nations. Siegfried Sassoon says this in his 1919 poem "Aftermath." Though it's set among the trenches of World War I, not the beaches of World War II, I believe it applies here and serves me well as an ending:

Have you forgotten yet? …
Look down, and swear by the slain of the War that you'll never forget.

Do you remember that hour of din before the attack —
And the anger, the blind compassion that seized and shook you then
As you peered at the doomed and haggard faces of your men?
Do you remember the stretcher-cases lurching back
With dying eyes and lolling heads — those ashen-grey
Masks of the lads who once were keen and kind and gay?

Have you forgotten yet? …
Look up, and swear by the green of the spring that you'll never forget.

Thank you.

Kenyon

From 1960 to 1964, I was a student at Kenyon College. Since 1987, I have been Writer in Residence there, teaching creative writing classes to sharp undergraduates. Along with an enduring love for the place, I have worries and concerns now for its future, recorded in the following pieces.

Kamp Kenyon's Legacy: Death by Tinkering

The Chronicle of Higher Education, February 2003
Adapted from a speech to the Council of Colleges of Arts and Sciences

Since returning 15 years ago to teach at Kenyon College, where I was a student in the early 1960s, I've becomc especially sensitive to change, to the costs and benefits of what passes for progress. I've reflected on life and on death, which comes closer with every edition of the Alumni Bulletin — my "Class Notes" inching toward white space and the necrology of "oldest undead graduate."

Lately, I've begun to sense the college's mortality, as well. I sense it the way the Admissions sales force talks of "making the class" — filling, maybe even overfilling the freshmen dorms. I sense it in curricular reviews that question what we do and don't offer. And I sense it in the shudder we in the faculty and administration feel at the talk of virtual classrooms and online degrees, at the possibility that this ever-more-costly private institution that holds classes only nine months a year — with its dormitories, playing fields, swimming pool, and tennis courts — is at best optional, at worst irrelevant.

Kenyon, like many liberal arts colleges, is a torn place. At current prices, we're obliged more than ever to deliver the goods, to turn out English majors who don't regard the apostrophe as an unidentified flying object. But that obligation is matched by another demand: to accommodate students in order to attract them to college in the first place. The result? We have both Kenyon College and "Kamp Kenyon."

I didn't coin the latter phrase or its spelling; the notion of Kamp Kenyon has been around 10 years, at least. It refers to that aspect of the institution that lets students get away with a lot, that coddles and gets conned. Kamp Kenyon deals with campus life and student problems: drugs, date rape, harassment, gender bias, dyslexia, dysfunction, angst, anger, homesickness, seasickness. It seems that bringing mere counselors, mediators, and advisers to our campus in Gambier, Ohio, and to other higher-education institutions around the country, is a growth industry. These people are thoughtful and hard-working, and much of what they do has developed in response to real problems. Yet I wonder whether their initially useful presence does not signal the piecemeal mutation of Kenyon College, and other institutions, into a therapeutic kibbutz — ultimately compromising the purpose of a college education.

Although Kenyon is about challenging and testing students, Kamp Kenyon is about serving clients. Kenyon keeps students busy; Kamp Kenyon makes them happy. Kenyon has rules, to which it makes rare exceptions; Kamp Kenyon has excuses, which then become rules. Kenyon trades in requirements; Kamp Kenyon trades in appeals, which become precedents, which become entitlements.

Kamp Kenyon manifests itself in small, seemingly trivial things that add up. For instance, several years ago, in the middle of August, faculty and staff members were invited to assemble in dormitory parking lots when the first-year students and their parents arrived. We were asked to greet them, help them unload their vehicles, and move things into dormitory rooms. I wondered whether I was the only one who flinched.

A couple of things bothered me. Envy was one. I came to college with one suitcase and a small electronic device. I don't remember whether it was called a "record player" or a "hi-fi," but the speaker was in the lid. These days, new students arrive looking as if they've looted Circuit City.

The other issue is more serious. When I first came to Kenyon as a freshman, I was required to attend a speech in the college commons by the chairman of the English department — eloquent, sardonic Denham Sutcliffe. The night belonged to him. His theme was making the precious time at college count, taking our studies seriously, regarding ourselves as professional students. I can still see him leaning back, pausing, and then proceeding to recite lines from Pope's "Essay on Man." The setting and Sutcliffe's voice, his style, his quality of mind seemed the proper frame for how a new student should encounter a professor. It's hard to imagine Sutcliffe helping some kid from Wilmette schlep bis sound system into the dorm.

But at Kamp Kenyon, we not only help students move in to their dorms, we help them move out of courses. Even though Kenyon allows students to drop or add courses a few weeks into the semester, and considers petitions for course withdrawal at any time, Kamp Kenyon has a mulligan rule: A student can withdraw from a course once before the senior year, without penalty, up to a week before the course ends. In my courses I have students on waiting lists. Is it appropriate for administrators to decide that a student who doesn't give a damn can bail out a week ahead of the final exam, while someone who earnestly wants to attend has been denied a place?

Kamp Kenyon's overly-accommodating approach continues through the end of the year. For example, with final examinations and papers approaching, April is considered a stressful time for students, especially those who have blown off the first 10 weeks of the semester. They're in a bind, all right. But wait a minute! The Student Affairs office now annually sends an all-campus e-mail message inviting administrators and faculty members to offer "comfort zones" for pressured students. A prize is awarded to the most ingenious entry. Last year, one office had a tableful of snacks and soft drinks. Outside a campus building, someone offered Popsicles from a cooler to passing students. Just next door, someone else had arranged for local masseuses to give in-chair back rubs to overburdened undergrads.

Kamp Kenyon's needs are huge, as is its agenda. We brag at Kenyon that we don't have a student union — the whole college is that. But recently we've been building student unions in disguise. A rickety old building that housed offices has been converted into a late-night theater and hangout. Plans for our new $60-million athletic facility show a movie theater, meeting rooms, audio-visual equipment, computers, a juice bar, and a pro shop. In an inadvertently revealing decision, a residence last occupied by Kenyon's provost will now be the home of an assistant dean of students.

Underlying all this coddling is the notion that students must have options — food options, athletic options, entertainment at all times — and that it is the college's obligation to provide and supervise such things. You might think, as I do, that a student can be left to his or her own devices at 3 a.m., to sleep, read, talk with other night owls, make love. That was the point of locating a college in a remote location in the Midwest, to escape from diversions. Now people are committed on behalf of the college to providing them.

In theory, I appreciate the impulse behind Kenyon's activities. I must say that it's possible that if I saw a couple of parents struggling with a half-ton sound system, I might pull into the dormitory and lend a hand. I might counsel and forgive a student with problems in my class. I might even have a chat about those memories of abuse and dysfunction that work their way to the surface in April, just ahead of papers and tests.

But the damnable thing about the administrative initiatives I've described is that they pre-empt such individual acts of kindness. They are the students' co-conspirators, their new best pals, figuring out ways through and around professors and requirements. The institution gets into the act, into what used to be the professor's field of force, and that diminishes us.

If a student has problems, I get an e-mail message — an issues-gram, I call it — from student affairs telling me that so-and-so is going through a bad patch, and my forbearance would be appreciated during this troubled time. What is the problem? I wonder, but in vain. Something like doctor-patient privilege has come between me and my student.

Liberal arts colleges remind me of those poignant cases you've seen on TV shows like *Live with Regis and Kathy Lee:* nondescript, nervous women bundled offstage for a makeover and returning an hour later, now happy about their hair, makeup, nails, and clothes. So, too, colleges attempt to make themselves over, with new buildings, summer-camp amenities, counselors, programs. They thrive on changes. But they should be reminded of what should never change, what must be kept out of the hands of the campus make-over artists: a true and vital engagement between the professor and the student.

This, then, is the death I picture for my small liberal-arts college — not dramatic but certainly lethal: death from tinkering. Death from accommodation. It's hard to say how it happened, when it started, who's to blame. But it comes down to this: In our attempts to attract students to Kenyon and keep them there, will the college itself become less worth attending?

Life and Death at a Liberal Arts College

Address delivered to Council of Colleges of Arts and Sciences Annual Meeting, San Francisco, CA — November 14, 2002

When I came to college — there's a room-emptying sentence fragment if I've ever heard one — when I showed up as a clueless, immigrant stock first-in-the -family-to-enter-college kid out of northern New Jersey, we were asked — make that required — to go to dinner in a place called Peirce Hall, the college commons, and there, sitting at long tables, framed by stained glass windows portraying great works of literature, surrounded by oil portraits of dead Episcopalians who were the college's founders and benefactors, there we confronted one of those men who — risking colleagues' sniping irony and contending with his own inner anger — incarnated the spirit of that time, that place: Kenyon College, September 1960. Denham Sutcliffe was the chair of the English Department and the night belonged to him. Making time count was his theme, this precious time at college, taking our studies seriously, regarding ourselves as professional students, in our works and days. I can see him now, a short, florid Oxonian, leaning back pausing and proceeding to recite those great lines from Pope's Essay on Man, lines that — I just realized — nicely summarize the trade of the deans and provosts I address today: "created half to rise, half to fall/ great lord of all things, yet a pretty to all/ sole judge of truth, in endless error hurled/ the glory, jest and riddle of the world." Kenyon College, Sutcliffe told us, was opening for its 136th year which — as time was measured in Knox County, Ohio — was a long stretch. But Harvard was beginning its 324th year and, in England, Oxford was well into its seventh century. The point was clear. When you came to college, you engaged with something that lived long and large, that measured, spanned and perhaps transcended time. A student's career was over in a wink — 36 months, and this was before junior year vacations became undergraduate perks. A professor's tenure ended quickly too, especially in Denham Sutcliffe's case. One of the duties of my senior year was to be his pallbearer. But our individual transience heightened his point — that we pass through college but the college itself remains, the college which belongs to us, as we belong to it. That sense of time is reflected in our rituals, our songs, our regalia, our buildings, our fundraising, our brochures and... some would unkindly suggest... in our curricula. You see it in the nervousness of first year students, in the shadowed poignance of graduates of fifty years ago, presenting themselves on campus one more, one last, time. Attending a liberal arts college is an act of faith, investing $100,000 or more in a liberal arts education is an act of faith and the core of that faith is the confidence that the college goes on forever. And that, just lately, is what I have been wondering about. And before getting to what's been weighing on me, let me suggest that if I am worrying, you should be worrying too. Ten years ago, in what appeared to be an act of career suicide, I wrote a non-fiction account of a year in the life of Kenyon College, *Alma Mater: A College Homecoming.* I taught a fiction writing seminar, lectured on recent American novels, followed hiring searches, took notes — or, at least, doodled — during department meetings, probed fraternity weirdness, feminist anger, alumni lawsuits, tenured anomie, and tenure-track angst and — in a move that should have gotten me a call from Stockholm — moved back into the same freshman dorm I had occupied in 1960. Through it all, I told myself I was writing about one place only, a singular place, Kenyon College, and what I came up with, no-holds-barred-warts-and-all-tough-love, would be about Kenyon College only. If I could get that one place right, that would suffice.

Then the mail came, mail from all sorts of places, lots of it from companion institutions in the Midwest liberal arts gulag, but there were letters from Princeton and Brown and from the Leeward Campus of the University of Hawaii. Over and over, one sentence appeared: if you crossed out the name Kenyon you could have been writing about our place. Kenyon's passions and tensions were shared: students concerned about cost — and worth — of what we taught; professors torn between teaching and research, the comfy prep school model and the cutting edge research university style — college as conservatory versus college as laboratory; administrators not sure whether all-around adequacy or jagged excellence was their goal, whether they should be keeping up with the pack or differentiating themselves from it. And this reminds me of the most exasperating trait I've come across in talking to people about their colleges. If you're discussing something fine and virtuous — delivering a compliment — people nod appreciatively, as if to acknowledge that the praise is not only merited but also has been delivered to the responsible party. If you risk criticism — grade inflation, oversized seminars, undergraduate grotesquerie involving the invariable trifecta of alcohol, drugs, sex — study the reaction. People look left, look right, look up the road at Harvard which, by golly — didn't you read about it? — has the same problems. Or down the road at a public institution where the problem is even worse. Sure, our students throw beer cans around, coming home late from parties whooping and cursing as they pass. But, hey, at

Ohio State they riot, they incinerate dumpsters after football games! The implication is clear: Our virtues are homegrown, our vices come in off the road, their symptoms are mild. To me this signals an unwillingness to straightforwardly consider the problem in front of us, on our watch, on our patch. That is what I aim to do now. I will speak of Kenyon but, considering that the institutional uniqueness is way overrated, I speak of other places too.

When you return to teach — profess — at a college you attended, you become especially sensitive to change, to the costs and benefits of what passes for progress. You reflect on life. On death. On your own death, which comes closer with every edition of the alumni bulletin, your Class Notes inching towards white space, towards the necrology of oldest undead graduate. Just lately, in addition to brooding on my own mortality, I have wondered about the college's mortality as well. Our long history notwithstanding, the seeming endless river of life that flows through us, and the weave of time and memory that we share, I sense mortality. I sense it in admissions, the way the sales force talks of "making the class," and in those periodic agony exercises — curricular reviews, outcome assessments — that question what we offer, what we don't. Oh for the straightforwardness of those DeVry ads we see on TV, smiling graduates in front of computers, peering into microscopes, carrying blueprints, all well-employed, assured that the money they spent at DeVry was well spent, education leading to higher income and a better life, all this while we send English majors out into the world ready to learn the meaning of irony the hard way, at Starbucks. I sense it in the shudder we feel at the talk of virtual classrooms, degrees online, the chances that all these trappings, these dormitories, playing fields, swimming pools and tennis courts, these ever-more-costly nine-month a year institutions, far from being morally and culturally imperative are at best optional, at worst irrelevant. It's the fear of giving a party to which no one comes.

So we have an institution caught between two obligations, a torn place. At current prices, we're more than ever obliged to deliver the goods, to turn out English majors who don't regard the apostrophe as an unidentified flying object. This we attempt to do at Kenyon College, and often we succeed. But the obligation to challenge is matched by another demand: to accommodate. And this has led to another institution, a burgeoning case of mission creep, something that is called Kamp Kenyon. That's Kamp with a K. I didn't invent the spelling or the phrase. It's been around for years, referring to that side of the institution that lets students get away with a lot, that coddles and gets conned. Kamp Kenyon is that part of the college which deals with campus life, student problems, drugs, date rape, housing, harassment, gender bias, dyslexia, dysfunction, disorders of all kinds, homesickness, seasickness, angst and anger. Its domain is almost everything that happens outside a classroom and, lately, some things that happen inside a classroom as well. It's a growth industry, it seems, bringing more counselors, mediators, advisors every year, people who take courses in dormitory life and student group management and non-alcoholic socializing and some of those people tell me that my book, *Alma Mater,* is on reading lists. Many of these Kamp Kenyon people are thoughtful, hardworking people yet I have been forced to wonder — and now I wonder aloud — whether their initially useful presence does not come close to compromising the purpose and point of a college education.

Here's the problem. Kenyon College is about challenging and testing students, Kamp Kenyon is about accommodating clients. Kenyon College keeps students busy, Kamp Kenyon makes them happy. Kenyon Colleges trades in requirements, Kamp Kenyon in appeals that become entitlements. Kenyon College has rules, to which it makes rare exceptions. Kamp Kenyon trades in excuses which become the rule. I want to be fair: much of this has developed in response to real problems and much that I deplore occurred with the consent of the administration, with the agreement — I'm tempted to say acquiescence — of the faculty. Another stab at fairness: notwithstanding my suspicion that rural, residential liberal art colleges are particularly prone to user-friendly compromise, let me avail myself of the fake left, fake right two-step I deplored just a minute ago: they have deans of excuses at Harvard, I am sure, and at many other colleges as well. Okay? But that doesn't stop me from worrying about the place where I live and work and the prospect of its piecemeal mutation into a therapeutic kibbutz.

Every year it's something else, some small something, trivial somethings that add up. A few years ago, in the middle of August, that time when the arrival of body-contact athletes signals the death of summer, I received an e-mail from someone I am sure believed in what he was proposing, that it was a good proposal, good per se and good for Kenyon and, besides that, fun. Faculty and staff were invited to assemble in dormitory parking lots when the first year students and their parents came in off the road. We were asked to greet them and help them unload their vehicles and move things into dormitory rooms. I wondered whether I was the only one who flinched. A couple of things bothered me. Envy was one. I came to college with one suitcase and a small electronic device, I don't know whether it was called a "record player" or maybe a "hi-fi." Anyway, the speaker was in the lid. These days, new students arrive looking as if they've looted Circuit City. Too much stuff, I think. The other issue was more serious. I tried to picture Denham Sutcliffe — that eloquent sardonic professor whose speech I just recalled — tried to picture him helping some kid from Wilmette schlep his sound system into his dorm. The way I met Sutcliffe — noticing his voice, that I can hear forty years later, his style, his quality of mind — seems to me the right way a college student should first encounter a professor. This parking lot aloha didn't feel right. Someone was trying to make the students happy. But maybe happiness isn't the first point a college should make. Or the last.

If you like helping students into dormitories, you'll love what came along later: helping students move out of courses. Like all colleges, Kenyon has a drop-add period that extends a few weeks into the semester. And, like other colleges, Kenyon considers petitions for course withdrawal at any time. This, somehow, did not suffice. A small human-scale place that advertises its careful review of individual cases decided that it was getting too many such petitions. So along came Kamp Kenyon's Mulligan rule. Once in a career — just once, for now, and before the senior year — a student can withdraw from a course, without penalty, up to a week before the course ends. Well, in my courses I have students on waiting lists. Am I right to feel my space has been invaded when someone decides that, for the sake of administrative convenience, a student can sit, mopey, medicated, manipulative, and bail out a week ahead of the final exam while someone earnest has been denied a place?

Now I come to another example of Kamp Kenyon's nibbling away at Kenyon College: comfort zones. With final examinations and papers approaching, April is held to be a stressful time, possibly for all students, most certainly those who've blown off the first ten weeks of the semester: they're in a bind alright. But wait a minute! Here comes an all-campus e-mail that invites everyone, faculty and staff, to offer "comfort zones" for pressured students. A prize will be awarded to the most ingenious entry. One office I walk through regularly has a table full of snacks and soft drinks. Ho hum. Outside a campus building, I see someone who is on the college payroll sitting in a folding chair next to a cooler, which she reaches into to offer popsicles to passing scholars. Just next door, down the road, someone else has arranged for three local masseuses to set up shop, giving in-chair back rubs to overburdened undergrads. And now I have to make one thing clear. I like many of my students. Whatever bad moods befall you, you can't make a career knocking students, not at a small college, without seeing your work, your life, turn sour. I like my students. I welcome graduation, yet seeing some kids walk across the stage, knowing I won't be having them in my life much anymore, drives a stake through my heart. I mention this because I refuse to concede to Kamp Kenyon's monopoly on the affection for, or from, students. The popsicle pushers haven't got a hammerlock on feelings. Another thing: I grant that it's possible if I saw a couple of parents struggling with a half-ton sound system, I might pull into the dormitory parking lot and lend a hand. I might. I might counsel and forgive a student with problems in my class; I might even have a chat about those memories of abuse and dysfunction which work their way to the surface in April, just ahead of papers and tests. And the damnable thing about the administrative initiatives I've described — the e-mails, the all-points bulletins, the camp counseling and scout-mastering — is that they preempt such individual acts of kindness. They are the students' co-conspirators, their new best pals, figuring out ways through and around professors, around requirements. The institution gets into the act, into what used to be the professor's field of force and, though some of my colleagues have welcomed this, I feel it diminishes us, it takes away from what we claim and who we are. It subtracts from me, when students take their troubles elsewhere. Granted, my degree isn't in counseling and all of us at small liberal arts colleges have learned that whole flocks of one-winged birds perch on our particular wire. Sometimes they flourish, sometimes they fail. It's hard to say. If a student has problems you get an e-mail — an issues-gram, I call it — telling you that so and so is going through a bad patch and your forbearance would be appreciated during this troubled time. What is the problem, you might wonder, but in vain. After 9/11, when lots of students were down and for some of them college-as-usual was too much to bear, e-mail informed me, and, them, that a college dean was willing to be "academically creative" at this juncture. Funny, I thought that was part of my job, in my classroom.

This list of peeves could go on in this vein. I won't, though. It gets worse. The college I attended was lightly endowed, i.e., poor, and its poverty enforced a kind of discipline and focus. There were things the college could not do so what it did do, it often did well. Now the college has enlarged, three times the number of students as when I attended, twice maybe three times the number of genders and much of this growth was to the good. I would not reverse it. Yet it is also true that diversity can divide, that to enrich a place is also to dilute it. This leads to a Balkanized — make that atomized — faculty, a student body less closely knit, with fewer common holdings. It's not just people that change; it's buildings also. Consider the Horn Gallery. It started as an old barn — an old wooden barn — that students took over and used for poetry readings, plays, art shows. It had some rough improvisatory magic but whatever else you said about it, one thing was unavoidable: it wasn't up to code. The administration responded with a new barn-like structure, fine, but someone at Kamp Kenyon decided that this building, this piece of college property, should be alcohol-free. Now granted, the laws of the state of Ohio which forbid under-21 drinking need to be obeyed. I grit my teeth and attend one grimly non-alcoholic event after another, wondering how many of the guests have "front-loaded." But to decree that not an event but a building should be alcohol free, now and forever, is presumptuous and invasive. It means that, after their fall and spring meetings, the college's own trustees cannot retire to a reception at the Horn Gallery. It means that adult writers attending the Kenyon Review's popular two week summer writing program are told — by college security — that they can't hold post-reading parties in the Horn Gallery and if they don't get that beer out of the refrigerator lickety-split, it'll be confiscated. It means that people who like getting married in the college chapel must take their toasts and their rental fees elsewhere. Keeping students happy has led to keeping busy the people who keep students happy and things have gotten out of hand.

Kamp Kenyon's needs are huge, as is its agenda. An article of faith at Kenyon — it's something we still brag about — is that we do not have a place called a student union. The whole college is that. But recently we've been building student unions in disguise. A rickety old bank building recently used for college offices gets converted into a late night theatre and hangout space. Plans for our new $60 million athletic facility have a movie theater, meeting rooms, audio-visual stuff and computers, a juice bar, a pro-shop. Early plans included a climbing wall as well. In an inadvertently revealing decision, a residence last lived in by Kenyon's provost will now be the home of an assistant dean of students. Underlying all this is the notion that students must have options — food options, athletic options, entertainment and diversion at all times, and that it is the college's obligation to provide and supervise such things. You might think — as I do — that a student can be left to his or her own devices at 3:00 a.m., whether to sleep, read, talk with other night owls, make love. That was the point of locating a college in a remote Midwest location, to escape from diversions. Now there are people committed — on behalf of the college — to providing them. In the name of happiness, a student's or a student's parents' happiness — we admit and readmit students with profound problems, serious disorders, suicidal tendencies — and to the extent we engage those students, we attract more of them, with results that are costly, sometimes tragic.

Our attempts to keep students happy misfire. We go where we should not go, do what should not even be attempted.

My final example is controversial. The jury is still out on our college court system, the intramural student-faculty-administration panel that hears and judges allegations of sexual misconduct, including harassment and rape. Is it legal? Illegal? Sub-legal? Quasi-legal? Para-legal? Why did we get into this business? The answer: to keep students happy. Any number of students, the argument goes, would not come to campus or would not stay were there no means of addressing offenses against them. To be sure, some of these offenses — rape, say — fall under the laws of Ohio, where the college is located and from which it has not seceded. But the implication is that the law of the land won't work, that even if lawyers don't brutally cross-examine, date rape cases, invariably compromised by under-aged drinking, will not prosper in local courts. Thus, we have our own system and thoughtful people who work hard to do the right thing. One doesn't envy them. It's terrible what students do, to — or with — each other, all our concealing notwithstanding. So now you get these cases. People try to keep things quiet, but it's a small campus and word gets around, rumors and whispers, sides forming, conflicting versions of events. Rashomon-like, and at graduation, students marching across the stage with ribbons on their robes, one color if you think your buddy got a raw deal, another if you think a girlfriend's complaint was mishandled. One recent case has led to lawsuits from both parties, the male who was expelled, the woman who left school, both suing the college.

This, then, is what it comes to, my thoughts of life and death at a small liberal arts college. This is the death I picture, less dramatic than what I promised but no less lethal: death from tinkering; death from drift, manipulation, self-assertion; death by accommodation. Hard to say how it happened, when it started, who's to blame. It comes to this: in our attempts to attract students to college and keep them there, will college itself become less worth attending? Liberal arts colleges remind me of those poignant cases one used to see on *Regis and Kathy Lee,* nondescript and nervous women bundled off stage for a makeover, returning an hour later, happy about their hair, make-up, nails and clothes. So, too, colleges attempt to make themselves over, with new buildings and new looks, summer camp amenities, counselors, programs. They trade in changes. But they need to be reminded of what shouldn't change — an engagement between professor and student that has to be kept out of the hands of the campus make-over artists.

I began with an account of a stirring speech I heard more than forty years ago, a passionate professor who conveyed the spirit and ethos of a liberal arts college. I end with an account of another speech, one that I make at Kenyon every year, near the end of summer. That sullen, succulent season is still warm when freshmen arrive for orientation and, after moving into the dorms, after the canoe trip, after watching *Ferris Bueller's Day Off,* which someone has decided is a college tradition, after all the deans and counselors say hello, after a battery of speeches in which the provost and president assure students and parents that they were students once as well, after a lot of wisdom about saying goodbye, saying hello, after all that, someone decides maybe it's time for a few words from a professor and so, like a pair of spavined old timers invited to toss out a ball on baseball's opening day, I join my colleague Perry Lentz, also a Kenyon graduate of 1964, to spend an hour discussing what is billed as "academic integrity."

The invitation comes from Kamp Kenyon, I'm happy to say, for I like a lot of people I disagree with and I appreciate that they give me this opportunity and also that they seem to have taken in stride my suggestion of a few years ago that, in a perfect world, many assistant deans and such would have found a more useful line of work, such as bread and pastry baking, landscape gardening, and full body massage. I'm now nine years older than Denham Sutcliffe was when he died and part of the charm — make that, the power — of a small college is that it allows the past and the present to connect with each other and with the future too. The future is this captive audience shambling into the auditorium in summer clothes, tardy and heavy-eyed and already talked damn near to death, which I now confront, just as Denham Sutcliffe faced the Class of '64. Put aside everything you've heard so far in orientation, I tell them, don't disregard it, just put it aside, the camping trip, the dormitory frolics, all the gooey bonding exercises. Put aside those likable Admissions people, for they are the college sales force and you are last year's sale. Put aside Kamp Kenyon, the counselors and all, for they are the local rescue squad and, although it's nice to know they're available, the less you have to do with them, the better. The things that brought you here are not the ones that will keep you here, if you stay. I've examined the records closely and can verify that no one has ever moved to Knox County, Ohio, because the food and sex were special. Put that aside and realize that your most important encounter with the college is with, well, you're looking at it this minute, the faculty. Check it out. The work that you do for us, with us, not the fun that you have, is your main purpose here. Forget all that welcoming oratory about how you may be the best entering class we've ever seen, with interests from A to Z, astronomy to zoology, so you should give yourself a standing ovation, just for showing up. They say that every year. What they don't tell you is about our failures, which are failures not because of lack of ability but because of indifference, insolence, complacency, and sloth. The fact that some of these hiders and sliders, these hang-dog half-assed characters, actually traipse across the stage at graduation doesn't eradicate the fact of failure, it just spreads the blame around some, compounding the guilt.

About professors. Some professors take attendance, some don't. Some call you by your first name, some by your last, with a mister or ms. in front. Some put chairs in a circle, campfire-style, and others stand in front of the class behind a podium, and call on people who haven't raised their hands, even though they are awfully busy taking notes. We have professors who think grading is more important, that once in your life you should be told whether your work's worth spit. Others find grading arbitrary, authoritarian, etc. Some professors are hard and others are easy; upperclassmen will provide names. The good news is that all hard professors aren't necessarily good and — oh happy day! — not all the easy ones are bad. There you have it. One size doesn't fit all and universal success — as Von Clausewitz said of perpetual peace — is a dream, and not a happy dream at that. Different as they are, difficult as they may be, there should be two or three professors who change your life here. You cannot bond with all of them, thank god. That would be too much to bear. But some of them, a few. And among the few there might be one who gives you the sense of knowing you, your vulnerabilities, your possibilities, better than you do, before you do. That kind of contact is what we offer, that kind of magic.

I'm sounding solemn now, I realize, so I mention three eccentric jihads which I repeat to you, in the hope that the campaign will widen and prosper: (1) a late arrival in class is ruinous and wasteful as an absence and should be penalized accordingly; (2) hats are out indoors and so are sunglasses for this is college, not the federal witness protection program; (3) don't yawn in my face. A human being, your professor, looks back at you when you sit before him. Cover your mouth when you yawn. Am I asking for the moon here? I go on a little more about reading that should be above the level of grammar school book report, i.e., I liked it, I couldn't relate to it, it bored me, about class discussions that should be more than an open mike session, "yeah, well, whatever," a self-serving show-and-tell period: I brought in a bird's nest, a Japanese officer's sword, a sponge. I talk about writing that should be focused and rigorous, not a random shake-and-bake of lecture notes and magic-markered quotations.

I'm near the end now, the end of my speech to them and my speech to you. I'm grateful for the chance to address incoming students. I know that out of this torpid late summer crowd, some good students will find their way to me, while some others mark me as a must-to-avoid. That's not bad for thirty minutes work. I am also thankful for the chance to speak to this audience of deans and provosts, though there'd surely be greater profit in listening. I've never understood why someone wants to be a dean or provost, what propels them, whether boredom and burnout in the classroom or the chance of intervening in the careers of their erstwhile colleagues. Did you jump or were you pushed? Is it a goal in itself or does it only work if it leads up, and maybe out, to something else? I wonder how things look to you and how you want them to be and I'd walk a mile in your shoes, any day, though it might be dicey. "If I ever set a murder novel on a college campus," I wrote in Alma Mater, "I'll make the provost the victim. Or more plausibly the killer." End of quote. I mean that as a compliment.

Now I take a deep breath and launch into my valedictory to the entering class and also to you. I end by telling them that the work they do at Kenyon College matters more than how happy they are at Kamp Kenyon and that the happiness they want should result from the work they do. And if they are miserable, unbearably so, they should leave, for every day at a place like Kenyon is a gift, every day they live at college they're in a zone of possible magic and if they don't agree, well there are economical life-style choices in Bangkok, Manila, and Luang Prabang I can recommend, where the cost of a college education could set them up for life. I like them, I assure them. But it wouldn't matter if I loved them. The idea of a small liberal arts college, endangered from within and from outside, is something I won't compromise. I hope that what matters to me matters to them, hope they will resist the nonsense that distracts them and the nonsense that is offered. I wish them all the luck in the world — I wish the same to you — and, on the way back across campus, I nod in the direction of my professor, Denham Sutcliffe, not yet forgotten, not quite, who is buried in a cemetery just up the road.

The Unthinkable Thoughts of Summer

Speech delivered to International Council of Fine Arts Deans

Fort Worth, TX — October 22, 2003

Is there anything like e-mail for inculcating a false sense of productivity? Not the sending of it, but the deleting of it as fast as possible. How much nonsense can I vaporize in a seminar break or better yet, in the length of time that I hold my breath? Job candidates auditioning in chemistry; fitness classes cancelled; stray dogs and wallets; rides to the airport; stern warnings from a college bookstore that needs to know, right now, what texts I'll be requiring in 2005; student colloquies, endless and inflamed. Then, in the midst of all this, like a rock in the river, there's a message that makes you stop and think. Early last fall, about the time my American Novel Since 1950 class was segueing from *Portnoy's Complaint* to *American Pastoral,* I got something like this: I'm sorry I missed your class which I take seriously, and I'm not copping a plea, but my horse came down with colitis and had to have emergency surgery in Columbus. It looks like she'll make it but I might have to miss the next class, too and I'll take whatever penalty you give me. I just wanted to let you know etc. etc. Well, the horse recovered. And the student, she wrote a decent final comparing the sex life of Updike's Harry "Rabbit" Angstrom to the sex life of rabbits, actual rabbits, and it's not often that I can get a female student to react thoughtfully to Updike. Happy endings all around but oh, the hours I spent wondering whether the email I'd gotten was a very new or possibly very old excuse; my horse broke down, right there with my puppy ate the homework. What should I do? What if the horse died? Or worse yet, relapsed and died while I forced the student to attend that second class? Would the absence be more excusable if the nearly fatal colitis had kicked in while the student was riding Seabiscuit to class?

You've got to love it, at least mostly love it, this daily blend of the sublime and the ridiculous. One moment you think you've heard it all — especially when it comes to student excuses — and then you're ambushed by a surprise. One day you're walking around in a world that goes back forever and will surely go on indefinitely and, a little later, you sense bad things headed your way, fast. For nine months, when I can spare a moment to brood about how old I am and how famous I wanted to be, I grant nonetheless that I am in a good, sometimes magical place and that lots of people would trade places with me, like the parents who accompany my students to class on visit days, the adults bursting with energy, bright-eyed, raising their hands, lingering after class, while their spiky-haired, heavy-lidded offspring pray not to get called on. This makes me wonder if the relationship between the people who profess and the people who pay couldn't be simplified: cut out the kids and meet, payer to payee, adult to adult.

Our life could be better. But it is good. Nine months of incredible clutter that discourages — mercifully discourages — prolonged reflection. Splash around in the shallows of a beach that's crowded and noisy, you don't worry about the drift of continents, the melting of ice caps, the slow grinding of tectonic plates. You worry about sunburn. But then, it's summer, when my thoughts go long and deep. Summer, that succulent season, that unwritten page that begins with graduation and ends when the football players come lurching into town. Summer on an empty campus is my time for serious wondering. Clearly the absence of students and faculty has something to do with thoughts of summer. But there's more, I believe. In the vision of empty paths and playing fields, locked-down classrooms, vacant commons, most of all the dormitories — that sound in fall like jukeboxes on which all buttons have been pushed, all songs playing simultaneously — dormitories, dark and mute and lifeless, in all this I get a picture of the nightmare which haunts me — us — all of us in the liberal arts, more especially those who do the liberal arts at small, residential places. The nightmare is this: those parents who sit in back of class may find themselves unwilling to finance an education that isn't vocational, that not only lacks an immediate job market reward but worse yet, all but guarantees that such a reward may never arrive, an education that insists, quaintly, that virtue is its own reward when the fact is that virtue may be its only reward. All those poets and writers, artists and musicians, philosophers and classicists we send into the world, enriched and impoverished from knowing us, our proxies, our products, our prides and joys. Can this go on? Should it go on? We give birth to them, litter by swarming litter every year. Why not send them straight to the animal shelter? Here's my dark vision, simply put: what if we gave a party and nobody came? Thinking about things like this is how I spend my summer vacation.

It's hard to contemplate change and loss in a place you love, especially when that very change and loss come packaged as something called progress. Last autumn, in an appearance before the Council of Colleges of Arts and Sciences in San Francisco, I tried setting out my sense of things, that is, what came to mind the previous summer. That speech, that kamikaze flight, was excerpted in *The Chronicle of Higher Education:* "Our Coddled Students: Kamp Kenyon's Legacy:

Death by Tinkering" — those were the headlines and this is what led to your invitation to me, that reposed in my inbox for quite a while before I said I would come. I hesitated… and with good reasons. In San Francisco, I began with a list of small things, the devil in the details: professors invited to help incoming freshmen move into dorms at the start of the school year, "the parking lot aloha" — and then, the Mulligan rule: students permitted to drop a class at no cost within a week of the course's conclusion. After that, "comfort zones" during exam times — baked goods, popsicles, in-chair massages, college-provided. There were more serious concerns, mainly about a beloved, often admirable college moving, whether by design or drift, beyond its most important function: the college going into the travel business with study-abroad programs, a.k.a. junior year vacations; the college going into the judicial business adjudicating rape and sexual assault cases; the role of the professor narrowing, of student affairs types increasing; all signaling the piecemeal mutation of an important college into a user-friendly therapeutic kibbutz. In our attempts to attract students to the college and keep them there, would the college itself become less worth attending? That's what I was wondering.

I was in Prague, thanks to my wife's Fulbright Fellowship, when my speech excerpt showed up in the *Chronicle*. In describing the college's reaction to the piece I have to specify that I can only discuss the reaction that I'm aware of, surely a fraction of the whole. And, I must add that the reaction is something I'm still discovering, in nods of approval, in sudden handshakes…and in silence, avoidance. By all accounts, the campus erupted in a firestorm of emails and phone calls, many of them angry. Angry at me, about me. Some people I didn't know, and I was pretty sure didn't know me, now hated me. To be sure, the administration kept its distance; a dozen faculty and administrators sent sympathy, sometimes condolence. All the alumni I heard from approved, as did numerous people at other places, where the piece was reprinted. But among current students, the reaction was mixed, shading from qualified agreement to bitter denunciation. I had suggested that some things about life at our college were not first-rate and that shattered the self-reinforcing détente between college and customer: I am here because I'm good, you are good because you're here, we are good because we are here together. And let the circle be unbroken, let the attitude, the assumptions, the booster pride and loyalty go un-interrogated. I was a fink, a whore, a mopey out-of-touch reactionary. Too often, way too often, the attention was directed not at what I said but where I said it, in the outside world, in a well-regarded publication. This raises an interesting question. Where does one take concerns about a college? To the trustees, scattered as they are, subdivided into committees, happy to be respected in a respected place? To the administration's senior staff? To the last five minutes of a faculty meeting, everybody numb and cranky, hoping that no one will raise his hand in the so-called open forum? To the Campus Senate, a faculty-student-administration body that spends hours discussing how to count beer kegs and what to do about bogus fire alarms? No way. To make your case locally is to be regarded as a local character in a company town, marginalized and condescended to. So I did what people said I shouldn't have done. I went public. That's public as in public relations, as in public relations problem. Forget the thrust and substance of my argument. Everyone was worried about its impact on the college, on the vision we have of ourselves. Everyone was a spin-meister, an image-doctor, media-wise.

In the months that have passed, months leading to another summer's reflections, nothing really has changed as a result of my speech. An added dash of irony, a little perspective, a heightened but still inadequate sense of the ridiculous are the most I can hope for. But the facts on the ground haven't altered. Just recently, a college which has employed lawyers to contended with litigation from fraternities defending their ancient claim on college housing has recently designated part of a dormitory as "gay, lesbian, trans-gendered, bisexual, queer and questioning" living area. Well, put me down as questioning, as in questioning whether a housing policy that frowns on one group and accommodates others is a coherent policy, whether it doesn't Balkanize the student body in the same way that the faculty is Balkanized. As for the name, one can only pray that Gary Trudeau doesn't hear about it. I'd hate to see my current employer, my alma mater, turning up — or into — a Doonesbury cartoon.

There's more. When Christmas rolled around last December, faculty were invited to help serve appetizers and punch at a student holiday dinner. "The students would enjoy seeing you in this informal setting," we were told, "and you are welcome to stay for dinner following." The hits just keep on coming, life imitating bad art. One more, I can't resist: Years ago, a wealthy trustee endowed a February event called — after the first name of Kenyon's founder, an Episcopal bishop, Philander Chase — Philander's Phling. Casino night was part of this year's theme and professors were invited to be blackjack dealers, tattoo appliers, coat check attendants, van drivers. Or we could just wander around "to help keep things running smoothly" (i.e., searching out and squashing delinquent acts).

What, I might ask, paraphrasing my students — what's up with that? What's up is that someone employed by the same college I work for, someone just as hardworking and well-intentioned, has come up with the idea that infantilizes and marginalizes the faculty, exalts student affairs honchos, and spoils students. "What's up with you?" I hear the retort coming back. I have no problems with parties and am willing to forgive a fair share of undergraduate grotesquerie. Midnight howling at the fraternity lodge behind my home, the occasional beer can in my driveway — I can hack it. But underlying all the changes I've mentioned, and many more that I haven't — trust me on this, they abound, they compound — is a change in the character of college life. Exceptions become entitlements, individually plausible changes become collectively subversive, faculty treated as bad cops one moment, addressed as party clowns the next. Well, if you teach what we teach, the humanities and the arts, you know that the character of the professor is crucial. In the sciences, hard and soft, this is sometimes the case. In the humanities, it is almost always so. What we are is as important as what we do and whatever lessons we teach — about traditions and innovations, style and substance — nothing comes before the urgent need to make what matters to us matter to them: our students, their parents. We don't convey information, we live it, we incarnate it. And if you happen to profess at a small college, your role as an exemplar, an avatar, is magnified, for what small colleges sell is contact with the professor, contact that is not confined to the classroom, not limited to office hours. See your professor at the post office, the bank, the bookstore, catch your professor browsing for bargains at Dollar General and Odd Lot, raking leaves, driving loser cars, there's no end to it. Students walking by professor's houses on recycling day can learn whether their kid is on chewable Prozac, who springs for Dom Perignon, who thinks Monsieur Andre will do just fine. These things are knowable and a certain amount of knowing is inevitable, part of the tight weave of life on a campus. Know your professor is a good thing only provided, as one stern Kenyon provost remarked, that the professor is worth knowing. Most of this is good, it's what brought me to a place like Kenyon as a student and brought me back as a professor, the flow of life through a beloved place, part Mount Olympus, part Grovers Corners. The chance for magic is constant and endless. And so is the risk of nonsense. The possible magic is that students will encounter a professor who will change their lives. Not every student with every professor, God forbid, but at least one or two professors for every student. If that doesn't happen over the course of four years, someone has been cheated or cheated themselves. So much for the magic. Now for the nonsense. The nonsense that demeans and dilutes, nonsense that, however well meaning, is misconceived and misplaced and threatens to turn us into something soft, amorphous, and not worth knowing. The first is what I referred to in my comments about Kamp Kenyon: that the proximity of professor and student is corrupted, turning the professor into a glad-handling, eager-to-please camp counselor. A colorful curmudgeonly character who turns out — surprise, surprise — to be your new best friend. I belong — and so do many of you, I can see — to the last generation to arrive in college fearing that they might not make it, they might return home as failures. Now things have shifted so utterly that those fears seem quaint. The institution, not the incoming student, is on trial; the college, the department, the individual professor all dread failure. Mediators, counselors, residential life experts, disorder experts of all sorts proliferate and the professor meanwhile — well, consider the last day of class, which once was stirring or poignant or a little bit sad because, let's face it, none of these kids will be in the same room with you again, not ever — and now the last day of class builds toward that moment, that spectacularly cruddy moment, when the professor is obliged to pass out student evaluation forms and then, in the interests of jury confidentiality, shuffles off while these forms are being marked and collected. Can there be any better evidence of how things have changed, how power has shifted? Of course, an administration has the right, make that the duty to keep tabs on professors and to solicit the opinion of students in this regard. But could they have found a more demeaning way to accomplish this goal? It's not enough to turn us into teamsters and tattooists. We must be waiters and waitresses as well, placing paper questionnaires folded like paper tents on restaurant tables. Was your order cheerfully taken, was the daily special clearly described, was the coffee hot, the restroom clean? It comes to this: professors are being coaxed into doing things they should not do. And what they should do — the most important thing they should do — is being surrounded by buffers, padded walls and safety nets, the perquisites of summer camp, rehab clinic, country club. And the saddest thing of all — what I did not mention in my speech last year — is that professors have acquiesced in much of this, collaborated in their undoing, whether in the interests of sloth, scholarship, or privacy, it's hard to say.

No one comes to a school because of its simpatico dormitory managers, its cool dean of students, its cutting edge alcohol and drug abuse counselors. The professor comes first, work comes first, and everything else — play, humor, sociability, life-long friendship, even — follows afterward. It accompanies work. It does not precede work, does not substitute for it. Residentiality is not a synonym for meltdown; small college proximity shouldn't propel a blurring of lines and roles, it should enforce them. Otherwise you get what Ring Lardner called "friendship ripening into apathy." In this grade-inflated, price-inflated era, and especially in the humanities, where we're always suspected of trading in airs and attitudes, a patty-cake reputation is no way to live. Or die. Unforgivable.

I'm almost done. In a rare act of administrative whim I was invited last year to join a committee, a "college marketing committee," chaired by the father of an incoming student, a fellow who was well known for assessing corporate identities, images, brand names. Our purpose, at least when we began, was to differentiate our college from others. What made us special, what made us — using the word loosely — unique. Bottom line: what did we have that might ratchet us a few inches up the greasy pole of success symbolized by the *U.S. News and World Report* annual college rankings? Here again, we see how colleges have gone from master to mendicant. "Will you be admitted to the college of your choice? Will you be admitted to any college at all? Are you, or are you not, college material? Those haunting 1960s tunes, oldies but goodies, have pivoted 180 degrees. The college is now the one concerned. Will the college be chosen, will it have a good yield, how low will it have to go — how deep into that problematic wait list, before it "makes" its entering class?

Now a confession: I like joining committees at my college, perhaps because I'm invited to join so few of them. Faculty meetings, department meetings — I'd rather have root canal work. But a fresh committee, chaired by an out-of-towner, a fresh cast of characters, meeting in summer — it might be fun. And there was, after all, an interesting question on the table: What makes us special, as special as we believe we are? That was the big question, well worth asking.

We never answered it. What we ended up doing — I strain to recall — was tweaking the website, considering whether we should recruit drama majors to lead campus tours to pump our spiel up a little. There was a survey that wondered about getting more "big name bands" to campus and creating fine-dining opportunities. Tweaks and massages in the comfort zone, like "we'll leave the light on for you" at Motel Six. The liveliest conversation was about increasing early admissions, which would lead to more acceptances, which would hoist our yield and maybe our ranking, etc. etc. as if everyone else in the liberal arts gulag weren't already contemplating, or already doing, the same thing, the same dubious thing. It was like the debates about poison gas in World War I, weighing a transient advantage over a lasting debasement. Whatever you could say about this idea, you couldn't say it was unique. Neither were the offerings around the table — our sports teams, our study abroad program, even our esteemed literary magazine. Nor our new science facilities. Nor our daunting $70 million super gym, a.k.a. "Fitness, Recreation and Athletic Center." Nothing special about any of that. Maybe nice, maybe necessary, maybe not… but not unique. Then I glanced around at the literature that covered the table, the brochures and self-advertisements of dozens of other colleges. Who were we kidding? They all featured the same handsome pictures, wise feeling and autumnal, multi-cultural kids walking down leafy paths, small groups huddled around caring teachers in coffee shops, laboratories, on the grass in springtime. Close friendships, careful teaching, small classes — we were all bragging about the same thing! Famous graduates, charming old facilities, cutting-edge new ones.

It's all good, as they say. Well, mostly good. It's the kind of institution, the kind of life I value and defend. But please, spare me the talk of uniqueness. It doesn't hold up except in one way. When I looked around the room at all of us on this college marketing committee and asked myself, why is this college special, the answer came to this and only this: I am here at this college. That's unique. That's special. Total solipsism, I admit and, in terms of committee's high-flown mandate, a mighty long run and a mighty short slide. But there you have it. I am here. This is my place, not some other place. And I grant that there are thousands of people at other places who might be thinking the same thing at the same time — though not, I hope, on a similar committee. That's all I could come up with and I saw no evidence that anyone else sitting around the table came up with anything more. Still, maybe it's enough. There is something in a liberal arts college that attracts and holds me, something worth having and worth defending, the importance of what we teach, the integrity and focus of the institution we serve. There are pressures all around, cultural and economic, that cannot be denied: the costs of college, the demands of parents, the needs of students, proliferating and escalating. And special pressure on the humanities, to show that what we teach is more than just nice to know; once again, the need to make what matters to us matter to them.

A constant problem, which we all contend with. I have no answer to this downward drift that besets us. Only three smallish suggestions: I would take a cue from the enthusiasm of parents on visiting day. Reach out to them, as well as to students. And break the unbroken rite-of-passage between high school and college. Encourage students to knock around the world before sitting at our feet. Chances are they'd have a deeper appreciation and a greater need for what we do. Another suggestion: consider whether turning out majors these days may be irresponsible, either because they are default majors, avoiding math, lab, foreign language; or, conversely, they are clones who head towards graduate school, a costly cul-de-sac for many of them, an outcome that obliges us to write increasingly guilt-stricken letters of recommendation for many years to come. Let's hear it for minors, those chemistry and biology kids who light up our classrooms, who are hungry for the chance to read and write, whose contributions to class discussion leave jaded, ring-wise English majors in the dust. Let's hear it for the business person who wonders who wonders what Updike is up to, whether Morrison is sizzle or steak. Let's hear it for the dentist who keeps *The New Yorker* or *The Kenyon Review* on his waiting room table.

But nothing will help more than being true to our purpose and keeping our employers true to theirs. What I offer, I realize, is no strategy. Sorry. It's a credo. But adherence to that credo — defining our roles, defending our work, defending our institutions — is our best hope. Delete those emails. Turn down those invitations. Postpone life-long friendships with students until at least a month into the semester. Grade honestly. Cast a sharp eye on the student whose sick horse kept her out of class. That's my way. It's not special. It is not unique. I hope.

Beyond

If travel were a meal, we could talk about appetizers and main courses. This about dessert: cognac and cigar and no rush to leave the table. *National Geographic Traveler* devised an issue celebrating fifty great places. My piece was the last. I was given a paragraph on "The Ocean." The biggest thing on Earth, confined to a paragraph! Who did they think they were? Or I was? Surprise: the piece was splendid. Now for my second and final offering, and unexpected service ace. Now my final offering. I love hot springs — outdoor baths where the water never turns cold. Idaho abounds in them, some well-known spas, others hidden away. I spent three weeks on — and in — hot springs. I'm glad I went when the going was good.

In Search of the Perfect Soak

National Geographic Traveler, Nov 2001, Volume 18 No. 8

I'm crossing the street in Council, Idaho, walking with Tim Hohs, the editor of the local newspaper, talking hot springs. A car stops in front of us, and my companion calls out to the blond woman behind the wheel. "Tell him about the springs you and your motorcycle buddies go to," he says.

"No way," she replies. "They'd cut my tongue out."

Another day, I am sitting in a restaurant in Stanley, contemplating a chicken-fried steak, talking hot springs again. Face flushed, the waiter leans forward. "There are no hot springs in Idaho," he says, wagging his finger. "None at all."

Sure thing, buddy.

Idaho has hot springs, all right — more than 200, in fact, according to a government list. Some are private and jealously guarded; others are run as businesses; still others are rickety and half-forgotten. No matter. I'm going to dip into as many of them as I can in two weeks time. Equipped with maps, guidebooks, newspaper clippings, and personal tips, I am searching for the perfect soak. I can't picture what the perfect soak will look like any more than Ponce de Leon could describe the Fountain of Youth he never found. But when I get there, I tell myself, I will know it. My first stop — on a twisting, back-roads route that will ultimately cover over 3,000 miles — is Desert Hot Springs, known in more raucous times as Miss Kitty's Hot Hole. Desert Hot Springs sits off a gravel road in southern Idaho, just north of the Nevada state line, at the bottom of the kind of boulder-rimmed cottonwood canyon that posses gallop through in Western movies. The place looks time warped, almost abandoned: a scuffed-up lodge, a cluster of cabins that Bonnie and Clyde might have stayed in, a well-worn swimming pool fed by pipes driven into a nearby hill. "When people come here, their jaws just drop as they look around," says proprietor Matt Olivas. "But if they stay one day, you can't get them to leave."

As the setting sun turns the canyon golden, and a breeze stirs the cottonwoods, I decide it's too late to drive on, so I check into a cabin. That night, everyone slips into the hot pool, locals and visitors alike, where conversation is relaxed and easy. As I settle into thermal bliss, savoring the dry desert air, tensions melt away, and I chat with Olivas, who is of Native American descent. His father brought him to these springs when he was five, he says. Decades later, his childhood memories of the place undiminished by time — he thought it magical — he came back and bought it.

Now, like other hot springs owners, Olivas speaks of his water the way Napa Valley vintners tout their wine. His water, he says, is thirst quenching, volcanic, naturally distilled, energizing, alkalizing, non-chlorinated, has low surface tension and natural fluorides. It flushes away fatty acids, hydrates, promotes health, and tastes sweet.

"There's nothing like it," Olivas says, "not Perrier, not Evian. The birds drink the water. Bees drown themselves in it. Deer come across the cold creek to drink in the pool. They know how good the water is."

There's a field of healing energy in and around hot springs, I'm told, and apparently it's detectable by dowsing rod. After Desert Hot Springs I find my way to Lava Hot Springs 200 miles away, a small 1950s-looking town with a state-run hot springs park, a place once sacred to local tribes who, legend goes, put war aside when they entered the pools. Later, people came by train to these waters, back before medical experts dissuaded them of the idea that waters could heal.

"I think M.D.s didn't want it happening," says George W. Katsilometes, a businessman, endocrinologist, and veterinarian who refurbished an abandoned sanitarium into the Lava Hot Springs Inn."They just wanted to give shots and pills, saying that healing water was all baloney."The town went into decline, but now, Katsilometes says, with the growing popularity of new approaches to staying well, there's renewed interest in hot springs.

After buying the sanitarium property, Katsilometes hired a man to walk it with a dowsing rod. He discovered hot water underground. My room in the inn overlooks the result: a complex of gardens and pools (five pools now and eleven more coming) filled with water that comes out of the ground at 144°F and hits the surface at 113° or so — about the limit for comfortable soaking. Now, just like in times past, people come here from near and far.

"We'll give them hot water, massages, whatever they need," Katsilometes tells me. "Wrap 'em up, slap 'em up, and they go home feeling happy."

Quite happy myself after a stint in the hottest pool, I move on. Burgdorf, Worswick, Baumgartner, Johnson's Bridge, Russian John, Elkhorn, Sunbeam, Slate Creek, Frenchmen's Bend, Rocky Canyon, White Licks, Laurel Mountain — the springs keep coming. To track them down, I stop at ranger stations, walk into campsites, hike into forests, and wade rivers. I find hot springs on hillsides, along ice-cold trout streams. Sometimes — improbably — I find them next to a busy highway. I park at the edge of the Craters of the Moon, 618 square miles of black lava and broken cinder, and climb down into a meadow where I find Wild Rose Hot Spring, a crystal-clear pool where I relax, soak, and float as trucks go barreling by.

By now, having accrued some experience and expertise, I have a clearer picture of the perfect soak. Though I've liked all the commercial hot springs I've visited — most of which are spring-fed swimming pools — I'm tantalized by the idea of a pool that isn't man-made, water that comes out of the ground un-piped, un-channeled, that waits for me un-welled, in a fine and private place where clothing is optional. That is what I'm looking for now, and I'm not looking alone.

The Provost of the college in Gambier, Ohio, that employs me — my boss, in other words — has agreed to join me for the second week of my 40-springs marathon tour. Ronald Sharp has a weakness for saunas and massages, I already knew, and I sensed he might step up to hot springs. What's more, Sharp is a former editor of *The Kenyon Review,* a literary quarterly, and a specialist in romantic literature. I could hope for some wise and stylish words from him.

Or not. Granted, in the early going he is dutifully Wordsworthian, remarking how hot springs combine "alpine fantasy and water fantasy." But after that, it's downhill. He regresses, spring by spring, toward childhood. "I don't care about curricular reform and language requirements," he exults. The academic novel he brought along goes unread, and he uses a volume of new poems by Philip Levine only to press the wildflowers he picks along the way. At times he seems disoriented, something like a stroke victim. He wants to visit gift shops and is fascinated by beef jerky and yard sales. One day I bring up a college issue. "I could give a damn," Sharp proclaims impatiently. "I'm like a lotus-eater. Just give me the springs." We are, I sense it, closing in on the perfect soak. North of Warm Lake, 16 miles down a forest service road, we find Sugah Hot Spring, a rock and masonry pool on the South Fork of the Salmon River, a basin of hot water beside a pine-lined river right out of Deliverance. Sitting in the natural pool, it feels like we are floating downstream, two men in a hot tub.

Another day we cruise the South Fork of the Payette River and enter a zone of magic in the Boise National Forest, near the town of Lowman. At Bonneville Hot Springs, some of the springs come out so hot — 185° — that the volunteer caretaker plants rocks in the stream flowing into the bathing pools to create cooling turbulence. The volunteer, Bob Rodin, a retired airline worker from California, is camping near us.

"In two hours I can have the pool in perfect shape," he tells me, a chore that can include hauling out bags of trash. His wife, Bobbi, has been enjoying the springs since age 12. "Hot water is the most healing thing on Earth," she says. "It removes the negatives. I come to catch up on my reading, to watch squirrels, and to converse with God."

Sharp and I feel we're on a roll. At Pine Flats Hot Spring, about 43 miles west of Stanley, which is 132 northeast of Boise, we find a geothermal waterfall, a wind-whipped curtain of steaming water coming off a stony hillside, raining on us, filling a pool at our feet. Could this be the perfect soak? I plead with the provost to pull himself together, appraise critically, evaluate scholarly.

"The whole experience is like being in a painting," Sharp begins, "but a painting with sounds, with smells, the shifting combinations of horizontal rivers, vertical forests, diagonal hillsides, some barren, some green, some snowcapped. And at the springs, there's this interplay between falling water and stillness, hot and cold — and wildflowers, everywhere."

While Sharp pauses, it occurs to me that we'll remember this trip for a long while. Our quest is eccentric, but is it any odder than pulling fish out of rivers, tasting wines, foraging for antiques? "There's a phrase in sports," Sharp says, resuming his soliloquy on soaking. "'Letting the game come to you.' You're not worried about time. You're living fully in the moment, with no intrusive thoughts about work or going to the dentist next week. All the mundane things fall away."

And what about the perfect soak? For all the springs we'd tried, there were dozens of others we didn't get to, springs reachable only by boat or day-long trek. For every site we crossed off, we added another to our list. The quest could go on and on.

Still, with so many springs under my belt, my image of the perfect soak has been further refined. Perfection is not to be found in the man-made pools nor in the natural hot springs, primal and undisturbed. (Nature leaves rough drafts everywhere: pools that are oddly shaped, shallow bottomed, overheated, awkwardly located or configured.) No, the perfect soak lies somewhere in between — a still wild place, not too hard to reach, improved by the human touch.

There comes a morning that Sharp and I are driving a dirt road along the South Fork of the Salmon River. We pull off to the side of the road, step into the Boise National Forest, scurry down a path to the river to find a hot spring. We have done this drill so often before, we take for granted now the smell of pine, the blitz of wildflowers, the clear, fast-flowing river. But this time is different.

At the bottom we confront an outrageous addition to nature: two rows of enamel bathtubs positioned between the hot spring and the river. Welcome to Molly's Tubs. An act of desecration, it seems at first, dumping old bathtubs in the Garden of Eden. But no, what we have here is ingenuity at its finest. Patches of rubber, weighted by stones, stop up the drains. We remove them, wash out the tubs with hoses that come out of the hot spring behind, replace the rubber stoppers, let the tubs fill.

Naked, we go down to the river to fetch cold water to blend with the hot. We feel wonderful, playing hooky from all life's time and trouble. We swear we'll return next year for sure, maybe even later this summer. Sharp mentions Huck Finn, and I can't blame him. We haven't discovered the Fountain of Youth. But, sitting in a forest, in tubs where the water never gets cold, we have come close enough for comfort, for joy.

Cry, the Beloved Casino

Rolling Stone commission, 1987, unpublished

"I ain't gonna play Sun City,
ain't gonna play Sun City."

★ ★ ★

I liked the early mornings at Sun City, those empty hours when the casino and the hotel, gardens and lawns belonged to security guards, dark sentinels who greeted the new day by shoving mirrors under parked oars, making sure that no bombs had been hatched during the wee hours of the South African night. The nights, too, were something to behold: Boers just want to have fun, English, blacks and Indians too. More later about those jingly, neon nights. But the mellowest time was dusk, because dusk was when I first saw the place and dusk was when I said goodbye to it, the day they deported me, and dusk is when stragglers come in off the Gary Player Golf Course, giving way to monkeys and baboons who crept out onto the greens while the last sunlight glanced into the volcanic crater in which Sun City reposes, South Africa's Las Vegas and its Tara and its Xanadu.

When a South African entrepreneur named Sol Kerzner first saw this empty crater ten years ago, he came in by helicopter, inspecting one of six sites proposed for a 170-room hotel-casino. One look at the place, Kerzner recalls, and he had "a clear vision" of what would be. His enthusiasm for the place hasn't deserted him: "It was right." He pictured a hotel, just where the first hotel was built, and the two hotels that followed — over 900 rooms — and the monorail that links them, the lake, golf course and gardens that surround them. He was like Brigham Young, glimpsing the Great Salt Lake.

Arriving years later, Steve Van Zandt, an American musician, member of Bruce Springsteen's E Street Band, saw what Kerzner had wrought. In quite a different light: a cross-the-border pleasure dome, Apartheid's playground, and it was largely through his efforts that Sun City became the focus of an international protest against South Africa's racial policies.

Sun City is the heart of the heart of darkness, a pariah casino-resort which — unfairly, it protests — has been made a symbol of racism. There's more. Sun City sits, like a maraschino cherry on a mudpie, in what is called the Republic of Bophuthatswana, an apartheid-created black-ruled enclave lightly-regarded by the international community.

And Bophuthatswana, like Venda, Ciskei, Transkai and other erstwhile "Bantustans" is the spawn of white-ruled South Africa, a would-be Australia with twenty million too many aborigines and no Paul Hogan. A boycotted casino, an unrecognized black state, an unpopular white one: the layers of controversy proliferate, like the verses in "A Hole In The Bottom of The Sea."

★ ★ ★

Sol Kerzner. King Sol. The Sun King. Empire builder, market operator, jet-setter. The tabloids love him: a high-flying, topsy-turvy, loose cannon of a man, thrice married, now reunited but not quite remarried to his third wife, a former Miss World. A vulnerable, shrewd, off-the-streets guy, belly out, chin forward, Kerzner is a clear case of life imitating art, bad art possibly, but Kerzner doesn't stick around for reviews. Son of Russian-Jewish immigrants, he started with hotels in South Africa, first one, then many: Sun Hotels. Then he moved into that peculiar zone of malleable black states in and around South Africa, places where vacationers could do things they couldn't do back home. They could gamble, take in an erotic movie, check out a T-and-A floor show. Rafting 'round the coasts of apartheid, an amiable Huck with a crew of amiable Jims, Kerzner operated in Swaziland and Lesotho, Botswana, Ciskei, Transkei, Venda. But the heart of his operation was Bophuthatswana and Sun City.

"That bloody video!" Kerzner burst out. A stocky, bull-like man, an amateur boxer gone to seed, he sits in his owner's suite, tie loosened, sleeves up, a hard-living man at the end of a long day. Tomorrow he flies to Israel, the day after to south of France. Now, though, he sits like a fighter on a stool, going into the late rounds of a touch match, hurt, angry, and not at all sure of getting a fair decision from the judges. "This is the one place in South Africa where you have harmony," he declares, "where you have no apartheid, where people live and eat and swim. That this place ought to get marked and attacked for apartheid — that's sick."

Once started, Kerzner is on a roll, anxious to be understood. How he was jobbed and jerked around on the Phil Donahue show, where he appeared opposite Steve Van Zandt. How Van Zandt "couldn't sell shit" before he mounted his Sun City campaign. How the Jesse Jacksons of the world use South Africa as a platform for self promotion. How Frank Sinatra, who inaugurated the 7,000 seat Sun

City Superbowl in 1981 was "the only guy who had the balls" to check out Sun City in advance, go ahead and play it, and never apologize afterwards.

After a while, Kerzner pauses. He picks at some shrimp and oysters, urges his guest to do the same. Then, out come his trademark worry beads, adopted to help break a smoking habit, a casino owner's rosary, dangling between his knees, fingers moving while he answers questions about South Africa, questions which — once you finish with talk about rock videos, about the bright future of Bophuthatswana, about how everyone on his staff smiles and it's impossible for anyone who's being exploited and enslaved to smile the way people around here smile — once you get through all that, you come to final questions of good and evil, and the worry beads belong. Kerzner knows that the final charge against Sun City has nothing to do with hiring blacks or training them or even letting them drink and gamble next to whites. The final problem, as Van Zandt says, is not what Sun City is but where it is, in a black homeland state manufactured by architects of apartheid, a cynical scheme designed to divide blacks into tribes and, by containing those tribes in homelands, disenfranchise them in South Africa at large. But that is the problem: Sun City takes a discredited corpse of a policy and pretends that not only is the corpse alive, it is also lovable. It even smiles.

"In 1948, when the national party came up with homelands, maybe it was a bad idea," Kerzner retorts. "All sorts of ideas are fraught with sinister... ideas. But now we're in 1987. There are a lot of black leaders who didn't ask for what they got, but then they said, we've got an option, we could make the best of it. Homelands meant apartheid in 1948, but we could produce something else, dignity and progress. Now you look around, you've got housing, schools, a university, community centers, you've got to be asking yourself, well, shit, who cares what the Nats were thinking about in 1948?"

So, though there is bad news all around him., Sol Kerzner forges ahead, a boy-child in his early fifties, many times a millionaire, planning new hotels like a kid visualizing a tree house: more hotels in Bophuthatswana, more hotels in Sun City, a whole series of hotels running up and down the surrounding mountains.

"We'll have wildlife!" he exults. "We'll have a huge bloody — I hate to use the word — theme park! We'll have several complexes. African theme! Amazon theme! Wild gardens, different birds, fish, all that shit! We'll have the biggest aviary in the world. Not enclosed! We'll get the birds trained. They'll be there!"

★ ★ ★

There are plenty birds already, swans, ducks, flamingos relaxing in pools outside the Bascades Hotel's Peninsula Restaurant and the only barrier I suspect is the invisible one — chlorine, they tell me — that keeps the wildlife from be-shitting the adjoining swimming pools, where kids splash down waterslides in the early afternoon while their parents sun themselves. Other vacationers wander among molded rock caverns, with bars and jacuzzis tucked in magic grottoes. Strollers plunge into a tropical jungle with waterfalls and fountains, rope bridges and rock gardens. Inside, service is attentive, waiters and waitresses never fail to smile.

"You feel a little like a missionary here, having seen the country grow and develop, having seen what you can make out of the people," Edgar Van Ommen says. "Basically, I believe in Sun City as much as I believe in God."

The speaker is Edgar Van Ommen, Austrian general manager of the Sun City Hotel. Van Ommen is one of a kind of foreign legion of European hoteliers, casino managers, food and beverage men who run Sun City and think of themselves as firm, fair-minded professionals — no racists — with lots to show and nothing to hide. They talk of jobs created — more than 3,000 jobs — and blacks, Tswanas, promoted to higher and higher positions, chefs, croupiers, and sent abroad for training.

"My biggest ambition is someday a Tswana sits in my seat," Van Ommen declares. It is as though the Peace Corps has gone to Oz. To be sure, the Johannesburg papers have the usual bad news: a hunt for ANC terrorists — "terros" for short — who have mortally wounded a constable; limpet mines damaging the rail lines between Johannesburg and the black township of Soweto; the National Party, in power since 1948, moving towards an election, nagged by the left, more seriously threatened from the right. But in Sun City, these read like reports from a war zone halfway around the world, barely audible in the Land of Smiles. For there is calm in the eye of' the storm, and profit. Although foreign visitors have dwindled, a declining Rand has kept South African vacationers close to home. Sure, the boycott was depressing, Van Ommen admits. But has it cost money? "Oh, shit no," he exclaims, laughing. "We made money like hell."

★ ★ ★

Sun City, Saturday night. The hotels are fully booked, the parking lots are filled by day-trippers from Joburg, blacks by the busload from Soweto. Kerzner said the time to see Sun City is on a weekend, "when it is really heaving." It's heaving now. In the Entertainment Center behind the Cascades Hotel the slot machines are hemorrhaging. To one side, the bleachers are full of bingo players. There are lines for restaurants, the curry tavern, the wild west saloon and, for people in a hurry, there's Greek carry-out, burgers, sausage, chicken, fish and chips. Movie-goers mill around outside the theater entrances, mulling over a Bayreuth-festival of x-rated cinema: *Erotic Dreams of Cleopatra, Naughty Girls Need Love Too.* Outside, on a balmy autumn evening the sidewalks leading to the Sun City Hotel and the main casino are a South African parade, black skinny kids, older blacks with beer guts and golfing caps, punks and prom-goers, sari-clad Indians, proper English-looking ladies who might be on their way to tea and scones, formidable slow-moving Boer vrouws in love with landscaping, amiable, hand-holding people, all. Inside the Sun City Hotel, a carpeted, mirrored alley feeds into the main casino, another packed house, blackjack, craps, roulette tables, many presided over by the haughty, competent black croupiers Edgar Van Ommen is so proud of having trained and promoted and in one corner is the Saloon Privee, reserved for heavy-hitting punto banco players, open as everything else, open to all, and just for a moment the gaudy egalitarianism of it all, black and white and neon, just begs you to believe what Kerzner and the rest would have you believe: you have seen the future and it pays. This is never more so than when, stepping outside the casino, you walk into a wall of sound, several hundred slot machines swallowing and spitting back out the coin of the realm, everyone playing, like participants in a gloriously wide open, only slightly-rigged election, and if these one-armed bandits were voting machines, Sol Kerzner would be making prize acceptance speeches in Oslo.

★ ★ ★

The dressing-room suite directly in back of the Sun City stage, right next to the suite Sinatra used, is a commodious place, nicely furnished, well-stocked with snacks and beverages, all in keeping with Sun City's now-shattered hopes of attracting world-class stars to the sub-continent. It's the sort of room you glimpse in opening shots of concert films, entourage kibitzing supportively while star paces back and forth, only a few yards away from an audience of roaring thousands. This is where I find Hazel Feldman, Sun City's entertainment director, a picture of despair and determination.

"South Africa and Sun City are very much the flavor of the month," she sighs. "It's just guaranteed headlines. I read that Joe Schmo turned down four million to play here and it's bullshit. Paul Hogan is saying he was offered two million. That's bullshit. He was never approached."

Frank Sinatra opened the Sun City Superbowl with two weeks of concerts, was paid a reported $2 million, awarded Bophuthatswana's Order of the Leopard and made an honorary tribal chief. And, though Sinatra came trailing controversy to a land which was fully supplied, Feldman doesn't regret the choice. "Sinatra was absolutely the right guy in the entire world to put a casino resort on the map," he says. In the years that followed, Cher, Shirley Bassey, Liberace, Queen, Glen Campbell, Rod Stewart, Elton John, Paul Anka, The Village People, The Beach Boys, Sha-Na-Na, Linda Ronstadt all followed. George Benson drew an audience that was 75 percent black. Sun City was on the map: that was its accomplishment, and its downfall.

"It's very difficult to say what turned the tide completely," Ms. Feldman reflects. It had always been tricky bringing entertainers to South Africa — distance combined with politics to keep them away. But in August, 1985, South Africa's President P.W. Botha made what is now known as "the Rubicon speech," in which he disappointed those who had hoped for fundamental reforms. Soon afterwards, a State of Emergency was declared. At the same time, U.S. entertainers mounted a campaign against South Africa. "Blatant, mindless, nothing short of intimidation," Hazel Feldman contends. "That's when management started asking is it really worth it — is it worth my client's interests to jeopardize their career — not because they felt they shouldn't come, they all felt the flack they'd get in the U.S. was not worth their clients career. That's for me when the wheels started to come off."

So who's playing Sun City, this Saturday night? In a mini-theater just off the Galaxy Video Bar, there's the Playmates Show, in which eight women — "We're your playgirls, living for today girls, going all the way girls" — appear in a series of topless tableaux. Introduced as Pepsi, Bambi, Volupta and so forth they impersonate French temptresses, naughty maids, women-in-prison, she-spiders, and the highlight of the show has the cast's one non-white performer, Ms. Desiré Bestman, writhing on a bed, lip-synching the roars of a lion. Down in the Sun City Auditorium a full house applauds "Movin'," a Las Vegas-style sequins-and-feathers extravaganza. It's a different story in the Superbowl, where a half-full house shows up for "Gymnastics Goes Hollywood," in which a couple U.S. Olympians, Bart Conner and Julianne MacNamara, preside over a show full of tumbling, stunt bicyclists, and a reprise of gold-medal routines from Los Angeles. Other recent attractions have included a magic show, ice-skating, a Wheel-of-Fortune giveaway, equestrian jumping, and a British sixties rock show. These are improvisations, Hazel Feldman grants, hoping that someday the stars will come out again.

"It's easy to sit 12,000 miles away and pontificate about how good it feels not to go to South Africa," she says. "Meanwhile, they clamor to go to Russia and Poland. It's a thrill to get to China..."

★ ★ ★

Afterthoughts

It would be wrong to make too much of my deportation from the Land of Smiles. I was in my hotel room on a Sunday afternoon, waiting to be called to a planned interview with Dr. Lucas Mangope, Bophuthatswana's first and, so far, only President. The President — whose government is half-owner of Sun City — had been advised of my coming and I, in turn, had been encouraged to request an interview. I was even looking forward to it.

Lucas Mangope's portrait is all over Sun City, in the hotels, the casinos, in the conference center that bears his name.

He is a dark-suited, dour-looking man with Sonny Liston eyes, shrewd and cautious and slow to smile. They tell me he avoids alcohol and tobacco, eats carefully — grilled meats and salads. They tell me that, although his nation is not recognized and his overseas visits have been limited to Israel and Taiwan, he faithfully attends the tennis matches at Wimbledon every year. In interviews, he condemns Apartheid, blasts South African heavy-handedness, and quotes Jesse Jackson with approval. And, though some people warn that he is a whimsical autocrat, a jailer of opposition politicians, a South African puppet, a union-buster at the platinum mines which are Bophuthatswana's leading source of income, there are others around Sun City who urge me to consider whether Mangope is presiding over a success story, a bustling, multiracial republic, an unrecognized African Camelot. That's the line.

The South Africa-created black states have horrible reputations: reservations, rural slums, labor camps presided over by tribal hacks who've sold out their own people for the sake of a title, a house and limo. But, in talking with staunch foes of apartheid, I'd noticed that Mangope and Bophuthatswana earned at least a dash of respect: the old man might be the best of a wrong-headed crew, his country the least pathetic consequence of an incorrigibly unfair partitioning of land between black and white. Now I am offered Mangope; like Kerzner, a man operating in the realm of the possible — a hemmed-in territory hereabouts. If he has created something halfway decent against bad odds, that would be worth knowing.

I scan a long list of questions for Mangope: the choices that he had, or didn't have, when he accepted "independence" from South Africa ten years ago; whether the seven discrete islands of land that make up Bophuthatswana might ever become something bigger, and better; what he felt when the radicals called him a Quisling; what it was like dealing with Pretoria, and not dealing with Washington; and — what all interviews come to — what it felt like to be Lucas Mangope.

A Sun City official, Peter Wagner, calls to tell me two Bophuthatswana officials want to see me in my room. I assume they are a pair of p.r. types, assigned to cheek me out before ushering me into the top man's presence. But when I open the door, I see how wrong I was. And I know my long list of questions is going to stay unanswered.

The dark-suited spidery man is Mr. J. Modetsi, Director of Migration. The big fellow in the leisure suit, the one who reminds me of George Foreman, is Colonel M.P. Nko, from the Border Control section of the Bophuthatswana Police.

They sit down, ask to see my travel documents, and are disappointed but not surprised to find I have no Bophuthatswana visa. Neither, surely, do the people in any of Sun City's 900 other rooms. This part is a charade. The next part is not. That's when they tell me I have been booked on a plane departing in a few hours and I'll be taken into custody if I'm not on it.

Grim-faced, they leave the room. And so, in a few hours, do I — evicted from the Land of Smiles. And followed: in Johannesburg, I'm met by a South African immigrations official who asks how much longer I plan to stick around. I tell him: not long.

★ ★ ★

The last day, I read the newspapers as usual, the same ones I saw daily in Sun City, where South Africa seemed so far away. That was Sun City's peculiar charm. In Britain, President Botha declares that blacks would never get majority rule and a black would never be head of state. "I believe in a Christian approach," he tells the BBC, "but at the same time I have never read in the Bible that to be a good Christian means I must commit suicide to please the other man." And, tucked away in the back pages of *Johannesburg Business Day*, this:

SA's annual white population growth rate slowed to 0.95% between 1980 and 1986, Central Statistical Services said.

Mid-year population estimates show the black population outnumbers the combined total of the other three race groups by nearly 11 million.

Total population is estimated at 28.4 million: 4.9 million whites, 2.954 million coloureds; 884,000 Asians, and 19.662 million blacks.

Demographers have warned that by early next century whites could register zero population growth...

Then — and now — it felt as though Sun City were quite far away. Farther all the time, a mirage, receding.

The Ocean

National Geographic Traveler, October 2009

On a ferry from Manhattan to Staten Island, on a voyage across the Drake Passage to Antarctica, on a copra-collecting ship nosing among tiny Pacific atolls, on a floating university circling the globe, it never fails. I stand at the railing, even though there's no land in sight; I stand there at night when there's nothing but stars, and I sense that there's something about oceans that I need, that everybody needs, something that a life spent wholly on land and inland would be missing. It has nothing to do with sunny, sandy beaches, diving, fishing, or purchasing coastal real estate.

The ocean puts you on the edge of infinity and eternity. It covers almost three-fourths of the Earth; it could drown Mount Everest; it generates perfect storms and total calms. It puts you in touch with the way things are and were, for even at this late date, every ocean voyage offers an excitement that's both ancient and childlike.

Standing at that railing, studying the horizon, something in you wants to shout "Land ho!" Like Columbus encountering America, Cook probing for a great southern continent, Magellan circling the globe, you feel some old and potent magic. And like them, you hope to discover a new world.

Paul Frederick Kluge is an American novelist living in Gambier, Ohio. He was raised in Berkeley Heights, New Jersey, graduated from Kenyon College in 1964, and has taught creative writing there since 1992. Kluge served in the Peace Corps in Micronesia from 1967-69. He frequently returns to his treasured places.

Also by P.F. Kluge

The Day That I Die Bobbs Merrill, *1976*

Eddie and the Cruisers Viking Press, *1980*

Season for War Freundlich Books, *1984*
Critics Choice, *1986*

MacArthur's Ghost Arbor House, *1987*
Critic's Choice, *1987*

The Edge of Paradise: America in Micronesia
Random House, *1991*

Alma Mater: A College Homecoming
Addison-Wesley, *1993*
University of Beijing Press, *2012*

Biggest Elvis Viking Press, *1996*

Final Exam XOXOX Press, *2003*

Eddie and the Cruisers Overlook Press, *2008*

Gone Tomorrow Overlook Press, *2008*

A Call from Jersey Overlook Press, *2010*

Master Blaster Overlook Press, *2012*

The Williamson Turn Vireo/Rare Bird Books, *2017*

CPSIA information can be obtained
at www.ICGtesting.com
Printed in the USA
FFHW021048241219
57228628-62750FF